CW00495426

WHY I AM A LIBERAL DEMOCRAT

WHY I AM A LIBERAL DEMOCRAT

Collected and edited by

DUNCAN BRACK

Liberal Democrat Publications

© Liberal Democrat Publications, 1996

Published 1996
by Liberal Democrat Publications
8 Fordington Green, Dorchester,
Dorset DT1 1GB. Tel. (01305) 264646

All rights reserved. No part of this publication may be reproduced, stored in a retrieval system, or transmitted, in any form or by any means, electronic, mechanical, photocopying, recording or otherwise, without the prior permission of the publisher.

British Library Cataloguing in Publication Data
A catalogue record for this book is available from the British Library.

ISBN 1 85187 308 2

Text set in Bembo.
Printed and bound in Great Britain by Redwood Books Ltd

CONTENTS

ACKNOWLEDGEMENTS

Thanks are due primarily to Trevor Jones, for responding so positively to my highly tentative suggestion for a new publication; to the Policy Unit at Party HQ for allowing me access to their database; to Graham Elson, Suzanne Gill, Sarah Gurling, Jo Hayes, Elizabeth Johnson, Judi Lewis, Andy Myles, Kate Parminter, Ben Rich and Celia Thomas for helping with names and addresses; to Andrew Hydon for mailing large volumes of letters; to Julia Smith for typing; to Hannah Doe for assistance with typography, layout and printing; to all the contributors, for making the publication possible; and to Andrew Reid and the Liberals of 1885, for going first.

March 1996 Duncan Brack

INTRODUCTION

In June 1885, the second administration of the Liberal Prime Minister William Ewart Gladstone, in power since 1880, was unexpectedly defeated on a vote on the budget. An election was set for the end of the year; extra time was needed for a new electoral register to be compiled following the significant extension of the franchise in the Third Reform Act of the previous year. The autumn of 1885 thus saw an unusually extended period of electoral campaigning.

In the months before voting took place in November–December, a journalist called Andrew Reid hastily compiled and published a book entitled *Why I Am A Liberal: being Definitions and Personal Confessions of Faith by the Best Minds of the Liberal Party*. It contained a total of 55 contributions from leading figures in the Liberal Party, ministers, MPs and many others, together with an essay by Reid describing the philosophy of the Party as he saw it.

I first came across this publication via a reference in Ian Bradley's excellent study of Victorian liberalism, *The Optimists* (Faber & Faber, London, 1980). Bradley believed that the contents revealed a marked lack of any consistency or consensus over the basis of Liberal beliefs. This was symptomatic, he argued, of the philosophical incoherence of liberalism at the time, caught in a period of transition. Gladstonian individualism was running into the sands, a development which became painfully obvious during the Grand Old Man's last administration of 1892–94. But the New Liberalism, which was to underpin the achievements of the great reforming governments of Campbell-Bannerman and Asquith in the next century, was still in its infancy.

I think Bradley was unfair. Of course the contributions to *Why I Am A Liberal* are diverse, as one would expect of any group of politicians, and particularly of Liberals. The tension between classical individualists and radical 'constructionists' is also discernible. But there is a very strong degree of consistency: over the moral (often religious) basis of liberalism; over the belief that the Party aimed to act in the interests of all, not just the privileged few; and in the conviction that a party committed to gradual change was the surest guard against violent revolution. Anyway, you can judge for yourself; extracts of Reid's book are printed later.

Why I Am A Liberal is not only of considerable historical interest; it is an enjoyable and revealing read. It occurred to me that a modern version of the publication might fulfil similar purposes in the 1990s. Somewhat to my surprise, Trevor Jones, the Managing Director of Liberal Democrat Publications, readily agreed. The result is the book you hold in your hands.

Note on contributions

Both members and sympathisers of the Liberal Democrats were asked to contribute to the collection. Some groups were obvious: MPs, peers, members of the Party's committees. Many of the rest came through my own contacts, built up during six years of holding the position of Policy Director for the Party. This was supplemented by suggestions from colleagues more familiar with sections of the Party than I am, such as the Welsh and Scottish Liberal Democrats. Responsibility for the selection, however, rests with me, and I can only apologise if the final result is severely imbalanced. If you notice that someone you think should have contributed is missing, remember that there's a good chance that they were asked and did not respond. If you think that *you* should have been asked, you could be right; make sure that Liberal Democrat Publications sells all its copies and I'll try and include you in the second edition!

March 1996 Duncan Brack

PART I

WHY I AM A LIBERAL DEMOCRAT

RT HON. PADDY ASHDOWN MP

Thirty reason why I am a Liberal Democrat:

1. Because Liberal Democrats believe that Britain's future success and prosperity can only be achieved by developing our greatest renewable natural resource – our people.

2. Because our first aim is to provide government which gives opportunities to every citizen to liberate their talents, skills and ability.

3. Because our vision is of a Britain of self-reliant individuals, living in strong communities and supported by active government.

4. Because we argue that success for Britain will only come if we are not frightened of change. But we do not think that anyone has all the answers.

5. Because we value experimentation, diversity and pluralism.

6. Because we think that cooperation ,balance and compromise produce a better chance for long term success than confrontation and single one-off ideological solutions.

7. Because we believe that Britain's current problems cannot be solved with short term solutions – if we do not take the long view, we will fail.

8. Because we believe that Britain's problems cannot be solved by Westminster alone, either. Success will depend on our ability to release the power, commitment and skill which lies within our communities to solve their problems for themselves.

9. Because for us, the concept of citizenship is central. But we see citizenship as a two-way street. Citizens have rights which must be defended; they also have responsibilities which society has a right to expect fulfilled.

10. Because Liberal Democrats know that no person is an island. We recognise the importance of the things we own in private. But we also know the value of the things we hold in common.

11. Because we believe that people are at their best as members of communities which care. So our policies are designed to improve the quality of life, to tackle poverty, to strengthen communities and to build up the common wealth.

12. Because when it comes to governments, Liberal Democrats like them as close to the people as possible.

13. Because we want governments to have as little power as they need, rather than as much as they can get away with.

14. Because we believe that government's first role is not to help people, but to help people help themselves. We prefer the hand up to the hand-out.

15. Because our aim is to create a political system in which the citizen has more power and the government less, and an economic system in which the stake of ownership is widened, the power of the consumer enlarged and the rights of the employee to share in the wealth they create asserted.

16. Because, in economic matters, we know that individual choice and flexibility are best provided through the free market.

17. Because we are suspicious about government interference, in economics as in everything else. But also:

18. Because we recognise that the market must be our servant, not our master.

19. Because we see government's economic role as setting the terms of trade, creating the conditions for success, making the investments the market will not make, breaking monopolies, encouraging competition and rewarding enterprise.

20. Because Liberal Democrats understand that we have a duty not just to ourselves but also to our successors. That is why we take the environment so seriously. But also:

21. Because we do not believe that we will save the environment by asking people to be more poor or less free.

22. Because our approach is to ensure that true environmental costs are built into the market so as to reward those who conserve and penalise those who pollute.

23. Because Liberal Democrats believe that there are two forms of equality which transcend all others. Equality of liberty and equality of opportunity.

24. Because we regard as inviolable the basic rights and freedoms of every citizen.

25. Because we assert every citizen's equal right of access to quality health care, welfare and education.

26. Because we have long been committed Europeans, believing that Britain can only be secure, successful, prosperous and environmentally safe if we play our full part in the new Europe which is now being built.

27. Because we are committed to strengthening global international institutions.

28. Because we reject outdated notions of national sovereignty, believing that they now stand in the way of common action against disease and hunger, the threat to the earth's life support mechanisms and the scourge of war.

29. Because Liberal Democrats alone understand this truth; that we cannot change Britain's future unless we change Britain's political system.

30. Because we are committed to electoral and constitutional reform and we shall not rest until the government of Britain is fully returned to the people it is there to serve.

Paddy Ashdown has been MP for Yeovil since 1983; he was elected Leader of the Liberal Democrats in July 1988.

RT HON. LORD JENKINS OF HILLHEAD

I am and shall remain a Liberal Democrat because it is the only party (together with its Social Democrat and Liberal predecessors) which has consistently represented my core beliefs, which I define as follows:I am firmly libertarian, sceptical of official cover-ups and uncompromisingly internationalist, believing sovereignty to be an almost total illusion in the modern world, although both expecting and welcoming the continuance of strong differences in national traditions and behaviour. I distrust the deification of the enterprise culture. I think there are more limitations to the wisdom of the market than were dreamt of in Lady Thatcher's philosophy. I believe that levels of taxation on the prosperous, having been too high for many years (including my own period at the Exchequer) are now too low for the provision of decent public services. And I think the privatisation of near-monopolies is about as irrelevant (and sometimes worse than) were the Labour Party's proposals for further nationalisation in the 1970s and early 1980s.

Roy Jenkins is the Leader of the Liberal Democrat peers and Chancellor of the University of Oxford. He was Home Secretary, 1965–67 and 1974–76; Chancellor of the Exchequer, 1967–70; President of the European Commission, 1977–81; and the first leader of the SDP, 1982–83.

RT HON. ROBERT MACLENNAN MP

Humanity is distinguished from the brute by the ability to curb the impulse to self-gratification if the indulgence of that impulse would inflict harm upon others. It is the duty of the individual to observe that limit upon his freedom and it is the purpose of civil society to organise itself so that the individuals who are its members are encouraged or constrained to observe that duty. Subject to that important distinguishing limitation, the liberal society is one which permits and fosters the full flowering of the individual human spirit in its glorious diversity. Democracy is simply a system for the organisation of society which embodies the notion that the ultimate responsibility for choosing who shall govern that society lies with the people.

Most modern democracies, unlike Britain, endorse the concept that the rules which govern the governors' decisions should also ultimately be determined by the people and set out in a constitution. Democracies, plainly, do not always foster the development of liberal societies. In the name of the people, they have, not infrequently, oppressed minorities and failed to permit and foster the development of the human individual. They have sometimes failed even to pass the first test of a civil society, that it should promote the duty of its citizens not to inflict harm upon others. After thirty years in public life I am wholly convinced that Britain should become a constitutional liberal democracy. This is our priority and why I am a Liberal Democrat.

Robert Maclennan has been MP for Caithness & Sutherland since 1966. He was parliamentary Under-Secretary of State, Department of Prices & Consumer Protection, 1974–79; Leader of the SDP, 1987–88; Joint Leader of the Social & Liberal Democrats, 1988; President of the Liberal Democrats since 1994. Currently spokesman on constitutional affairs and national heritage.

ALEX CARLILE QC MP

No nation, however great or small, can truly be regarded as just or even civilised unless it is prepared to guarantee the basic rights of its citizens. Once, those rights might have been limited to imposing a duty upon the state to guarantee life and liberty. In a modern society we are surely entitled to expect a more generous and fruitful relationship with those who govern us. A right to liberty of life and speech remain fundamental, but to those we should now add that it is a fundamental freedom of the citizen in a society like our own to enjoy a reasonable quality of education, decent health care, publicly supported housing for the needy, and respect for the elderly who are an increasing proportion of our population. In my judgment liberalism in the context of a democratic state is the surest way to provide a guarantee that the state will meet these standards.

Alex Carlile has been MP for Montgomery since 1983. He was elected Leader of the Welsh Liberal Democrats in 1992.

JIM WALLACE MP

In autumn 1971 I responded to a party political broadcast given by Jeremy Thorpe and Lord Byers. Together with a membership application form, the Scottish Liberal Party HQ sent me a copy of Russell Johnston's pamphlet *To Be A Liberal*. I read it, found that I agreed with much that was in it, and promptly joined up.

The Liberal Democrat values which I most cherish are individual freedom, social justice, tolerance and a sense of community.

To me, the liberal society is one which exalts the individual and does not lose sight of the individual man, woman and child when policies are being developed. It follows from that, that if each individual is to achieve his or her potential, they should not be enslaved by ill health or by the lack of resources to feed and clothe themselves, provide a decent roof over their head or afford them quality educational opportunity.

Furthermore, any society which respects individuals must be tolerant of each individual and his or her right to be different. All this is to be seen in the context of people living together in a community and having responsibilities towards each other, and not simply being citizens who demand and exercise rights.

Put very simply, alone on a desert island, one has maximum opportunity to exercise freedom; but without being able to relate to other individuals, I believe that one's proper individuality cannot develop.

The form of government a society possesses must provide a framework for these principles to flourish; hence my commitment to decentralisation and, as a Scot, to the establishment of a Scottish parliament. Nations, however, like individuals, must act cooperatively and work for the common good of the community of nations.

Although it sometimes seems an uphill struggle, I believe that time is on the side of the values which our Party represents.

Jim Wallace has been MP for Orkney & Shetland since 1983. He was elected Leader of the Scottish Liberal Democrats in 1992.

JACK AINSLIE

In 1945, whilst still in the army, I voted Labour and I'm not ashamed of having done so. By 1950 I had become totally disillusioned by the top-down socialist approach of the Labour Government, even though it had quite properly acted on the policies of two great Liberals, Beveridge and Keynes.

Early in 1950, talking to a friend about my dilemma over whom to vote for at the forthcoming General Election, he said 'What about the Liberals?' and waxed eloquent about the Yellow Book, cooperation, profit sharing, employee participation and, of course, the central focus of freedom and the individual. Even in that unlikely political climate he convinced me. I had found my political home and have remained a Liberal, now a Liberal Democrat, ever since!

In the early 1960s I found inspiration in Jo Grimond's vision of leading a radical non-socialist party of the centre-left. It turned me into an activist and was also why I welcomed the emergence of the SDP and campaigned vigorously for a merger of the two parties.

I won a county council seat from the Tories against all the odds in 1964, at a time when Liberals were looked on as ineffective do-gooders. I was determined to do my bit to change all that and soon took a chairmanship in a basically Tory authority to prove that Liberals could take hard decisions when they had to, but not lose their commitment to work for and with individuals in society. I'm glad that I did so. Just look where Liberal Democrats have got to in local government now!

It may have been a hard 'row to hoe', but I don't regret for one instant my decision to join the Party and work for it over thirty years.

Jack Ainslie was a farmer, 1951–95; Wiltshire County Councillor, 1964–93; Education Committee Chairman, 1973–77; County Council Chairman, 1985–89; parliamentary candidate, Devizes, 1974, 1979; European candidate, 1979, 1984.

JOHN ALDERSON

Police officers are forbidden to take part in party politics and I agree that this should be so, but the police function is a political one and by 1982, I could no longer contain the political impulses which demanded an airing. Consequently I resigned the police in order to campaign as a Liberal, later Liberal Democrat.

I am a Liberal Democrat firstly because my instincts are liberal. I am an implacable opponent of political extremism, having witnessed in my lifetime the human suffering which it has caused. Extremes of the political right and left have more in common with each other than either has with liberalism.

I am a communitarian at heart, and an advocate of constitutional reform in Great Britain by reason.

John Alderson was a policeman 1945–82; Chief Constable, Devon & Cornwall, 1973–82, Assistant Commissioner Metropolitan Police, etc.

JOHN ARDAGH

I first worked with the Liberal Party in 1951 when at Oxford, and I continued to support it thereafter. Then in 1980 I eagerly backed the 'Gang of Four'. I knew David Owen personally and admired him, and I hoped that the SDP might really break the mould. What a sad outcome followed! I have since always backed the Lib Dems, but sometimes without great enthusiasm.

Four reasons why I am a Liberal Democrat:

1. Above all, *Europe*. I warmly believe in a tightly united Europe,with EMU, open frontiers, common political and defence policy, social chapter, etc. The Tories are appalling on all this, as we know; and though Labour's policies sound better, I do not trust it not to backslide when in power. The Lib Dems have the most coherent and positive attitude to European integration and to Britain's role at the heart of Europe.

2. *Leadership.* I have always liked the Liberal and SDP leaders, not excluding the unfairly-treated Jeremy Thorpe. Paddy Ashdown is clearly the best party leader around at present. Blair speaks well, but is too much the slick toothpaste salesman to be convincing. As for Thatcher and Major, ugh! It's a pity that the Lib Dems have so few high-quality leaders to back Ashdown up:but this will change once the party has more MPs and is able to attract more new people of high calibre.

3. *Class.* The Lib Dems are the least class-based party and they cover the widest spectrum of the nation. Blair may be wooing the middle class, but much of his party remains stuck in outdated working-class attitudes. The Liberal Democrats are best placed to heal the damaging class divisions that have ancient roots but were much worsened by Thatcher's vindictive feud with the unions. These divisions make us a laughing stock in Europe.

4. *Proportional Representation.* It is of course a negation of democracy that a party with 20 to 25 per cent of the vote should get 2 to 3 per cent of the seats. Again, it makes us a laughing stock abroad. The Lib Dems are right to press hard for PR – not only in their own interests, but in those of creating at last a genuine democracy in this country.

John Ardagh was born in 1928 and educated Oxford; formerly on staff of The Times, The Observer, *etc; author of many books on modern France., Germany, Ireland, Europe, notably* France Today, *still in Penguin.*

JOYCE ARRAM

As a teenager I was so 'left' I made Marx look a moderate! I was so blinkered that my idea of free speech was that only the Labour Party had the right to be listened to. The public should not be contaminated by hearing or reading other parties' policies. What changed this attitude? A party political broadcast by the Labour Party, given by Dr Edith Summerskill MP, and then attending a ward meeting of our local Labour Party where I took exception to being addressed as both 'comrade' and 'sister'. Ridiculous but true!

I started to look around, listen and read what the other parties had to say. Clement Davies was Leader of the Liberal Party. This was in the mid 1950s – pre-Eric Lubbock's spectacular byelection win at Orpington. I liked what I heard from the Liberals – worker participation, site value rating, involvement of people in their own future. Proportional representation came into my accounting much later. I wrote to Party HQ and they put me in touch with our local party in St Pancras (now Camden). I got involved in helping neighbouring constituencies with council byelections – particularly in Finchley (now Barnet) where I survived a canvassing initiation of being doused in water, chased by dogs and kidnapped by the local Young Conservatives. Politics were *fun!* But I realised there was more to it than the fun – we could change the world for the better and I wanted to be part of this.

In the early 1960s I was elected Chair of St Pancras North Liberals and candidate for the first GLC elections – all in the space of a few weeks. This was followed by being a sub-agent in the 1964 general election and adoption as parliamentary candidate to fight the 1966 election (SE Essex).

When the SDP was formed I resented their claim to the centre – we were already there. But by the time the merger came I realised it had been necessary for the SDP to exist for us to re-evaluate our own policies and attitudes. The public realised that 'centre' politics did not mean ineffectual policies and that two parties could work together, admittedly on occasion with acrimony, but we could and did work. We also know how to compromise – it was time for fusion.

So what is so special about our Party which makes us different from the others? The opportunity to progress and have a say in its policy-making – not just at conference but on working groups formulating policy. Our ability to conduct a democratic debate and ensure that as far as possible all points of view are heard – even if the result may not be exactly what you wanted. Yes, there are still areas for improvement and policies I do not necessarily agree with. We are not afraid of proposing policies which we believe are for the greater good but are to our personal detriment, eg our 1p on income tax to go towards the cost of education. We are prepared to accept an increase in tax – less money in our pockets – but we know it will be properly spent in investing in the country's future.

Joyce Arram is Secretary, Liberal Democrat Lawyers' Association; formerly Liberal parliamentary candidate (SE Essex and Ruislip Northwood constituencies); founder member Liberal Democrats. Legal executive by profession – council member, Institute of Legal Executives.

LORD AVEBURY

The central idea of liberalism, to me, is the equality and dignity of human beings. Mr Gladstone's famous peroration, in one of his Midlothian speeches, about the sanctity and inviolability of the life of the hill villagers of Afghanistan, finds an echo in modern liberalism's unwavering support for human rights all over the world, and the determination that human rights should be a weightier determinant of our foreign policy, as compared with commercial and consular considerations.

The end of the 20th century is an era of unvarnished greed, and the lottery culture has infected government to the extent that everything is done for the immediate material gain it secures, largely for a few jackpot winners. In our foreign policy, this means sacrificing principles for the benefit of large UK companies, particularly those engaged in the arms trade. While the Iran–Iraq war raged, at a cost of hundreds of thousands of lives, we did a roaring trade with both sides, while pretending to observe an embargo. Now those markets are lost, but we are repeating the same mistake with other autocracies like Saudi Arabia and Indonesia.

This policy prevents Britain from playing an effective role in promoting human rights. Sometimes we cave in abjectly to the pressure from dictatorships which happen to be good customers, but more usually there is a more subtle reluctance to criticise, when to do so might damage our commercial interests. That was very obvious when, year after year, Britain was one of very few states which abstained on resolutions against South Africa at the United Nations.

When I first entered the Commons in 1962, I became Secretary of the Parliamentary Civil Liberties Group, dealing with human rights in the UK. After 1964, when the chairman, Anthony Greenwood, became Minister of Housing, I took his place, and continued to hold office until 1970 when I lost my seat. That experience taught me that we have no grounds for saying that Britain's record is perfect. We may criticise the Chinese gulag, the *laogai*, but our own prisons can be guilty of appalling abuses, like the shackling of pregnant women. In the sixties, the Civil Liberties Group tried hard to call attention to abuses of the rights of Catholics in Northern Ireland. We were not allowed to raise discrimination in housing or employment in parliament, on the grounds that those were matters for the Northern Ireland parliament at Stormont. That should be remembered when the Turks are under fire because they prohibit discussion of Kurdish human rights in their Grand National Assembly.

Liberal Democrats do not have a monopoly of wisdom on these issues. We have to work together with those of like mind in other parties, and we are ready to concede that here, as in many other aspects of government, many Conservative and Labour supporters share our attitudes. Perhaps because of our history, and particularly our experience on the Irish question, we appreciate that cooperation rather than confrontation is often a better way forward. That does not mean that when there are real differences of principle, as there have been so often recently on home affairs, we should not put up a robust opposition. It does imply that we have to be ready to consider entering into coalitions, as is perfectly normal everywhere else in Europe. I believe that the Liberal Democrats have a duty to break the silly taboo against coalitions, and to break the stranglehold of minority rule which has lasted far too long.

Eric Avebury was the victor of the Orpington byelection in 1962. He was Liberal Chief Whip from 1963–70 and has been Chairman of the British Parliamentary Human Rights Group since 1976.

HELEN BAILEY

It started a long way back, when I was very young, and I think then that I was influenced by my father (a staunch believer in liberalism even in the dark days of the '70s), his liberalism and probably the family's nonconformist Christian roots.

As I have grown up, my views have become clearer and more focused and having spent some time thinking hard and long about life and politics

I have returned to those views, which are about justice and an appropriate way to order society, rather than being simple political tenets and values.

For me, the belief in the uniqueness, the rights and responsibilities of every individual is crucial, but unless it is balanced with a belief in the value of 'community' or 'society', the belief in the individual tends merely towards 'survival of the fittest' and becomes selfish and self-seeking. Similarly, to concentrate on the society without recognising the individuality and very different needs of the people who compose that society is too inflexible, too lacking in freedom and too likely to create a society in which people are made to be square pegs in round holes and lose their own willingness to contribute.

A Liberal Democrat society is one, it seems to me, in which we all have the opportunity to hold our own destiny in our own hands. That destiny is not simply about our ability to make money and gain material enhancement. It must also be a society in which we are able to choose our priorities, whether they are about physical, spiritual or material enrichment, as all are valued in terms greater than the purely economic. We understand, however, that within that society our individual aspirations and achievements impact upon those of our neighbours and the fellow members of every community in which we participate, and recognise our duty not to impede them in their own fulfilment. We also recognise that people have a right to be supported in their lives, especially when they are, for whatever reason, particularly vulnerable, and that this should be a social duty, not carrying stigma or reluctance. Society should give willingly to those who need from it, knowing that any of us may be in that position and that a healthy and free society is one in which the fear of loss of income, ability or capacity is not an overriding inhibition.

We extend that sense of contributing to the world in which our communities are located, knowing too that we (as human beings) are not the sole occupants of this world, either in space or time, and that our behaviour toward our environment not only impacts on the fellow occupants of our world here and now, but will continue to do so for the rest of time.

Essentially, it seems to me that the ideal lies in recognising the common humanity of all of us, and accepting and rejoicing in the understanding that we all have the capacity to contribute, and the need to receive, within the many communities in which individually we play a role.

Helen Bailey is a member of the Federal Executive and Federal Policy Committee, active in promoting women, training candidates and in the Association of Liberal Democrat Councillors.

MALLEN BAKER

Several things crossed my mind when, having left the wilder shores of the Green Party, I considered where would be my natural political home.

I remained convinced that the greatest challenge facing mainstream politicians across the world is that of integrating ecological concerns with the day-to-day priorities of creating wealth and security. In every country decision-makers are talking about how to create a sustainable society, but nowhere yet does one exist. We know that we need to achieve it, but frankly, we don't know what it will look like when we succeed.

So my first realisation was that green politics could no longer afford to marginalise itself on the fringes with high-minded ideals untempered with the reality of political influence. Sustainability has to become mainstream pretty fast if the human race is to survive the next century.

The second was the realisation that the Liberal Democrats are committed, as a party, not just to the environmental concerns of green politics, but to many of the more political aspects as well – such as providing a framework within which people can release their full potential, bringing power down to a level where people can exercise it for themselves, and establishing a political constitution which allows full representation at each level of decision-making.

Then there was the leadership question. Paddy Ashdown had consistently impressed me with the clarity of his understanding that the environment needs to be at the heart of economic policy above all other, and that the party needs to be committed to sometimes controversial measures such as ecological tax reform. The Party continued to prioritise the environment, even as it slipped down the political agenda during the recession.

That leadership was enormously influential. But the party had to fit as well. There are two other decisive factors from a green standpoint:

The party should be free from the control of vested interests. Measures to achieve sustainability will demand sacrifices of us all, and whether it be the interests of the City and the large corporations or of the trade unions, policies that deliver a healthy environment cannot be held to their veto.

Most importantly, the party must have the courage to make its case. Elements of the green programme are good populist politics, but some are about facing the difficult decisions. A party that hides from this will never be able to deliver genuinely long term policies in government. Over the last five years, the Liberal Democrats have shown themselves prepared to take risks for the right reasons. The Party has refused to play the tax-cutting game that has been demeaning political debate in the UK for the last ten years. At the last election, it promised to raise a tax for education, and found itself rewarded for its courage when the promise proved to be popular.

So even though there will be times when greens will be frustrated that the urgency understood by some within the Party is not understood by all, or that the election campaign doesn't succeed in pushing the boundaries quite as far as they could do with being pushed, still it seems likely that for a long time to come, the Liberal Democrats will be the natural political home for those greens who are serious about politics.

The only danger will be if we start to take that fact for granted and forget it is a privilege which needs to be earned.

Mallen Baker is the editor of Challenge, *the political journal of the Green Liberal Democrats. Before joining the Liberal Democrats he was one of the two Principal Speakers of the Green Party, and a Green Party Co-Chair.*

CLLR JACKIE BALLARD

I was recently described by a friend as a 'conviction Liberal' and I think that was fairly accurate. As long ago as I can remember I have been involved in some form of political activity – probably starting with opposing the Vietnam War, the Miss World competition and nuclear weapons and moving on to working as a social worker in the East End of London, campaigning for a toy library in rural Somerset, complaining about school class sizes and the destruction of the NHS.

I didn't find a political party which I wanted to join until 1985, when I was convinced by my local MP (Paddy Ashdown) that I was a Liberal and that I had something to contribute by belonging to the Party – I suspect he was just trying to divert me from writing so many letters to him about all the issues which concerned me in Thatcher's Britain!

Only then did I learn about the Party's policies and philosophy and discovered that I had been a Liberal all my life without knowing it. The legacy of 16 years of a mean-minded, destructive Tory Government is that many people think that 'there is no such thing as society' and that the only way to survive is to think only of oneself and immediate family. I firmly believe that, with encouragement, people can be generous and fair-minded and can work together in communities to build a better society.

I have not always agreed with all the policies of the Liberal Democrats and I am less enamoured with the free market than are some other members. I think the state has to provide the basics of opportunity – education, health and housing – for those who cannot fight in the marketplace with their vouchers and charters. I don't come from a privileged background myself and know that many people don't have the self-confidence to jostle to the front of the queue. There will always be those who need a helping hand.

At no time have I considered or would I ever consider joining another party – there is no other party which has the same commitment to civil rights, to building strong communities, to empowering people, to decentralising power out from Westminster, and to the European ideal.

The best compliment I ever had was from someone who said: 'When I want an instinctive Liberal reaction to a question or policy, I phone Jackie' – I think that was rather too flattering, but I would like it to be true.

Jackie Ballard is the PPC for Taunton and a county councillor in Somerset; she was a member of the Federal Policy Committee, 1990–95, and is a member of far too many other things to stay sane and healthy.

LORD BANKS

I am a Liberal Democrat because I believe in a world order based on justice. For this reason I support the United Nations.

I am a Liberal Democrat because I believe in regional groupings of nations and support the European Union.

I am a Liberal Democrat because I believe in social security and I support a social security system based on helping those most in need.

I am a Liberal Democrat because I support an economic system centred on a free market influenced at vital points by the state.

I am a Liberal Democrat because I believe in steps to deal with the flaws and threats in the environment.

I am a Liberal Democrat because I believe in partnership in industry between management and labour.

I am a Liberal Democrat because I believe in individual liberty and I want to see introduced a Bill setting out our individual liberties.

I am a Liberal Democrat because I believe in Home Rule for Scotland and Wales.

I am a Liberal Democrat because I believe in fair voting and support proportional representation with the single transferable vote.

Lord Banks is a former President of the Liberal Party and Chairman of the Liberal Party Executive. He was Liberal Deputy Whip, House of Lords, 1977–83 and spokesman on social security, 1975–89.

LIZ BARKER

Because woman's work is never done and is unpaid or under-
paid and it was a Liberal Government which gave married
women property rights and a Liberal MP's private member's
bill which removed the terror of backstreet abortions from
thousands of women and was an important step on
the road to economic independence which is
a cornerstone of personal dignity
and
because I was brought up a Scot, but my dad was English and

in 1974 the SNP was shouting that 'It's Our Oil' and making the emotional appeal that we shouldn't be ruled by Westminster when we were always getting gubbed at Wembley, but nobody could tell me if I would need a passport to get back from visiting my grandma down south; I came to the realisation that national aspirations for Home Rule are legitimate, but racism, whatever its guise, is abhorrent and must be actively opposed

and

because being pro-European is not a deliberate attempt to subvert national identity but the way to ensure that the horrors of the last world war are never again a reality

and

because freedom and liberation are rarely won by individuals, rather by groups of people joining in common cause to achieve change, but organisations of whatever sort have a tendency to be oppressive; it is preferable to be involved with a party from a proud tradition of social reform and which is committed by its constitution to the eradication of injustice and the pursuit of liberty

and

because if there is to be an environment and a society fit for people to live in for years to come, politicians have to have the courage to think and say the unthinkable today

and

because private medicine is an obscenity which has no place in a society as wealthy as ours, and if the NHS is to survive it depends upon the support of politicians committed to the motivation and vision of Beveridge

and

because the hallmark of a civilised society is the way it treats its minorities, and we're all Jock Tamson's wife's bairns; the only politics worth being involved in are those which seek to unite and celebrate diversity in the interests of the common good

and

because the Labour Party has divested itself of the best of its socialist tradition, leaving voters with a choice of conservatism or conservatism unleaded, and I want radical and fundamental change for all women and men

and ....

for lots and lots of other reasons I am a Liberal and a member of the Liberal Democrats.

Liz Barker joined the Liberal Party in 1979 and was sabbatical chair of the Union of Liberal Students in 1982–83.

GENERAL SIR HUGH BEACH

There is some difficulty for me in saying 'Why I am a Liberal Democrat' because in strictly party terms I do not belong to any persuasion. I accepted the offer to work on a statement of defence policy because I was looking for some constituency which would adopt a middle way in the nuclear field between unilateralism and the *status quo.*

Why has the British attachment to nuclear weapons proved such a durable feature? The crucial decision to acquire nuclear weapons was taken in the Stalin era by a Labour government, almost as a reflex response: to stay at the 'top table' and not feel too feeble. The story that Ernest Bevin came back from the United States, after being treated by Byrnes with inadequate respect, saying that Britain must have the bomb 'with a bloody great Union Jack on it' is well-attested. But even if apocryphal it exactly catches the mood in which the government of that day took its decisions.

Since then the nuclear weapons programme has been maintained and developed both as a result of military inertia and because of the political paralysis induced by nuclear weapons being used as a weapon in domestic politics. Conservatives have supported nuclear weapons partly because they believe in them, but equally because the Labour Party, or parts of it, from time to time has declared itself unilateralist, allowing the Conservatives to play the popular tune of accusing the Labour Party of giving away the country's ultimate weapon, and so to win elections. The Labour Party has repeatedly given up the idea of getting rid of nuclear weapons, and agreed reluctantly to keep them, in order to defend themselves against the Conservatives. As a result of the endless repetition by all parties of the unprovable thesis that nuclear weapons have kept the peace, or that we must hold on until everyone else gets rid of them, any departure from this doctrine has become a certain vote-loser. This issue has become a weapon in domestic politics which has no parallel in America, France, China, Russia and probably not in other marginal nuclear countries. A kind of collective political cowardice has meant that in the UK there has been hardly any serious re-thinking of nuclear issues at all.

I entertained the hope that Liberal Democrats at least would point out that this is not an all-or-nothing situation. The British Trident force as currently planned could absorb a great deal of reduction, in terms of missiles and warheads, while still retaining formidable deterrent power. The right thing to do is to press for multilateral negotiations towards proportionate and mutual reductions among all the five permanent members of the Security Council (being the five avowed nuclear weapons states). In their latest policy paper (*Shared Security*, 1994) the Liberal Democrats seem to have got this bit pretty nearly right.

Sir Hugh Beach is a retired general. His last job in the army was Master General of the Ordnance. He is now Vice-Chairman of the Council for Arms Control

LORD BEAUMONT

I am a Liberal Democrat because the Liberal Party to which I belonged and belong joined with the Social Democrats. But I do not know what a Liberal Democrat is because I do not know and never have known what the Social Democratic Party was. I suspect – and this is the only time I remember agreeing with Cyril Smith – that it should have been strangled at birth. I still find it hard to forgive David Steel. Nor (with the one dazzling exception of Shirley Williams, who is the best politician since Jo Grimond) do I find that I have much in common with Social Democrats.

What I am is an Ecological, Egalitarian Liberal.

I am a Liberal because I was converted to the Party by Frank Byers when I went up to Oxford in 1949.

I am a Liberal because I grew up in politics under the leadership of Jo Grimond.

I am a Liberal because both my grandfathers were Liberal MPs in 1906.

I am a Liberal because, as John Pardoe crystallised it, the hatred of Tories is the beginning of wisdom and to be Old Labour was to be centralist and undemocratic and to be New Labour is not to be on the side of the poor and afflicted.

I am an Egalitarian because I care passionately about the misery of the poor and because I can spare some pity for the rich who do not stand a camel's chance of reaching the Kingdom of Heaven unless they can be forced to disgorge their riches.

I am an Ecologist because I know that we must live in harmony with the planet or perish.

I read that leading Liberals have been influenced for the most part by Mill, followed by the trio of the Bible, Keynes and Schumacher. Mill rings no bells with me, but I gladly lay claim to Jesus of Nazareth, the Old Testament prophets, Maynard Keynes and Fritz Schumacher as my major gurus.

Tim Beaumont was Chair of the Liberal Party 1967–68 and President 1969–70. Made a life peer in 1967, he is currently Lords spokesman on environment: conservation and the countryside.

RT HON. ALAN BEITH MP

What makes us different?

Put simply, we are alone in our determination that social justice shall be achieved in a liberal democracy: that fairness and freedom shall go hand in hand. Most striking of the differences between us and other parties is our attitude to power. We are in the business of changing the relationship between individuals and communities and the structure of power. We want to give people more power over their lives. And it is because we recognise the dangers of concentrated power and are determined to control it that we are more entitled than others to insist that it has to be used to increase social justice and protect the environment. We can advocate the use of state power for specific social purposes which do not feature on the Tories' agenda because we are committed to controlling how it is exercised. We see in local government how comfortable the Labour Party is with concentrated power, and how unwilling they are to see its use by them put under any restraint.

The truth is that each of the other parties regards its views and policies as more important than democracy itself. It is not that they do not, for the most part, have a theoretical acceptance of democracy – it is simply overridden by their conviction that they are right, and that democratic procedures are in the way of important benefits. If democracy has to suffer in the cause of advancing conservatism or keeping Labour in power it seems to them a price worth paying. To us it is a price neither they nor we are entitled to pay, because it is a cheque written on the hard-pressed and hard-won fund of freedom, which belongs to us all.

We already have the policies to express this fundamental value. A fair voting system, a written constitution, a Bill of Rights, freedom of information, genuine democratic local government, devolution of power to the nations and regions of Britain – they express vividly and in practical terms the values which clearly mark us off from the other parties.

– FROM 'LEADERSHIP FOR FREEDOM', HEBDEN ROYD PUBLICATIONS, 1988

Alan Beith has been MP for Berwick-on-Tweed since 1973. Liberal Chief Whip 1976–85, he is currently Deputy Leader of the Liberal Democrats, spokesman on police, prisons and security, and election manifesto coordinator.

MIKE BELL

Underlying any political movement there are a set of assumptions and values which make up its political philosophy. This exists at different levels within the party:

- The level described in the preamble to the constitution – a written version which represents the results of negotiation between the various wings of the party.
- The unwritten set of assumptions which underpins the policies which emerge from the deliberative policy-making process.

- The unwritten assumptions contained in the policy responses and pronouncements of the spokespeople (mainly the Parliamentary Party), in the media.
- The written and intellectual 'political philosophy' of those who write on such matters (often referencing previous writers).
- The unacknowledged assumptions of the ordinary party member – the reasons they feel a sense of resonance or sense of belonging in the Party.

Of course, if asked 'what is your political philosophy?', most people would not know how to reply. The answers can be deduced from the way people vote or from their views on a range of questions.

For the political movement to succeed, there are two preconditions:

1. There must be harmony between the various levels of political philosophy, or at least between those elements which communicate to the electorate.
2. The assumptions and values must represent the aspirations of a reasonable percentage of the electorate.

If these preconditions are met, ordinary campaigning, luck and an absence of scandals will ensure success.

In the Liberal Democrats in 1996 these conditions are still not met. While there is a good 'fit' between the constitution, the policies and the values of ordinary members, three outstanding inconsistencies remain:

- Local campaigning is often populist rather than inspired by vision.
- Spokespeople too often pander to the media or express personal views or constituency interests.
- Intellectual and written versions are still dominated by 19th century 'liberalism'.

It is because I do believe that the political philosophy represented by the constitution, much deliberative policy, the actions of the best local councillors and the values of ordinary membership does represent the aspirations of many people in the country that I remain a Liberal Democrat.

I hope to continue to make some small contribution to developing and promoting the real political philosophy of a Liberal Democracy, replacing the demonstrably inadequate version of liberalism, and working towards the harmonisation of spokespeople's pronouncements and campaigning with that philosophy.

Mike Bell joined the SDP when it was formed, ran SDP Greens, has been influential in pushing the Lib Dems in a green direction and was a member of the Federal Policy Committee, 1990–94.

DAVID BENEDICTUS

Why I am not *a Liberal Democrat*

– Well, I was. And a Liberal before that. It seemed the only party to put principle above self-interest. Easy, some said, to have principles when you have no hope of power but I didn't agree. A certain moral absolutism is essential if one is to lead rather than follow. At university I had toyed with the Tories, but when Selwyn Lloyd, the Foreign Secretary, speaking to us in the Oxford Union at the time of the Suez Crisis, assured us with tears in his eyes that there had been no collusion between Britain, France and Israel, and when just a matter of weeks later it appeared self-evident that he had lied, I shook the Tory dust off my hush puppies and looked elsewhere. The trouble with Labour was that it would not, perhaps could not, make up its mind. On Europe, on Vietnam, on unilateral disarmament, on nationalisation, on private education and health, on all the major issues of the day, the socialists dithered disastrously. And while they dithered inflation rose to 30 per cent, and Britain teetered on the verge of bankruptcy.

So that seemed to leave the Liberals, and later the Lib Dems. The innocence of the third party, under Jo, Jeremy, David and, briefly, Bob, was endearing; I for one wanted more innocence rather than less. But the association with the Gang of Four was the end of innocence. To hop into bed with those who were clearly putting self-aggrandisement above principle was whoredom.

Paddy did his best. But when I was coopted on to the arts and broadcasting working group and saw the Lib Dems from the inside of Cowley Street I was distressed. Factionalism, functionalism, irresolution, a desperate desire to placate rather than to lead the voters meant that by the time that policies for the manifesto had been agreed upon they were so diluted as to be anodyne. Only occasionally did I feel proud to belong. Once when the Party announced that it was worth putting up income tax by a penny to pay for education (I was reminded of Churchill: 'There is no better policy for the future than putting milk into babies'), and then when Paddy went to Bosnia and (recently) to Yeovil to find out the truth at first hand – these were admirable initiatives.

Because, you see, politics is straightforward for a third party. You say what is right and you do what you can. You proclaim the essentials: fairness, tolerance, integrity, generosity, caution and concern, and you apply these essentials to such issues as may arise. You put world issues before domestic ones; you put domestic issues before party ones; you put party issues before personal ones, and you do not apologise for these priorities. Having decided on your policies, democratically, but ideally with the full support of your leader, you set these out in plain English at conference. And when called upon to address matters of principle in the Houses of Parliament or in the constituencies, you do not waste time slagging off your opponents. You ensure that your own standards of integrity are shared by your councillors, and, if and when they are not, you act promptly to disenfranchise those who have discredited you.

You are honourable, broad-minded, consistent, and persuasive. You speak with a single voice. You need not then be surprised if the voters flock to you. You are, after all, giving them what they want – moral leadership, lucidly conveyed. And your only real problems begin when, as a result of such policies, you find yourself in power – but that's another story.

I seem to hear the response of the Party upon reading what I have written in this brief essay. 'But you are describing exactly what we thought we were doing.' Really? Then as soon as it becomes obvious I shall rejoin the Party – although by then I shall be one amongst millions.

David Benedictus is a writer and director for stage, TV and radio; Commissioning Editor, Drama Series, Channel Four, 1984–86; Readings Editor, BBC Radio Four, 1989–91; Editor, Drama, BBC Radio Three, 1993.

VIV BINGHAM

In 1981 I used four words to summarise an answer to the question 'What is it to be a Liberal?' Fifteen years on, with a new name and constitution for the Party and its members, I still believe they synthesise for me why we endure (or enjoy) the slings and arrows of the unremitting and often unsuccessful toil of third party political life.

We are *universal*. There are timeless beliefs and values in our credo – liberty of the individual, freedom of expression, equality of opportunity regardless of race, ethnic origin, gender or sexual orientation – which we believe can and should apply throughout the world.

We are *local* in applying those beliefs. Individual freedom leads to commitment to communities. Most people will gain their identity by belonging to and participating in a locality, a town, a workplace. Only as these local identities are recognised can the outward devolution to districts, counties, regions, states and international federations be sensibly created.

We are *practical*. We want to make structures work in a way which fulfils people: works councils to end destructive divisions in employment and ensure economic success and social responsibility; open, accountable government so that everyone can take part in it; education and training at every age so that people can participate fully in economic, social and democratic life.

We are *visionary*. We foresee the needs of a changing world and prepare for them – less full-time traditional employment; higher proportions of elderly people; new threats to personal security, health and safety, and to the environment; and many others. Our answers will not be short-term, populist reactions. We will positively build a society where collective action – be it pollution taxes, community policing, responsible overseas aid or any other policy – enhances both individual freedom and thriving, caring communities.

Keynes and his collaborators in the Yellow Book of 1928 borrowed some words from the New Testament to explain it: 'Our aim is not the perpetuation or perfection of this or that mechanism or system, but that individual men and women may have life, and may have it more abundantly.'

As a party, we must win to achieve these aims. and we still have too many Jeremiahs, Eeyores and (even worse) 'quick fixers' around. We are on a long march to radically change the world, and sometimes I've been sustained by the words of a not very radical Liberal MP/poet, Hilaire Belloc:

From humble homes and first beginnings
Out to the undiscovered ends,
There's nothing worth the wear of winning
But laughter and the love of friends.

Whatever else our party is, its comity has always been more important than its committees; and its laughter and friendship are without parallel. That's why I'm happy and proud to be a Liberal Democrat.

Viv Bingham has been unsuccessful candidate for the Liberals/Liberal Democrats at Euro, Westminster and city elections. He was President of the Liberal Party in 1981–82, and more recently Regional Chair for the North West (1992–95). He has been known to sing peace movement songs.

SIR WALTER BODMER

I have been a Liberal and a Liberal Democrat essentially all my adult life. My preference for the centre was, I think, instilled into me by my mother and grandmother. I have always disliked the squabbling between the extremes of left and right and felt that the liberal approach provides the balance with which I am most comfortable. I do believe that some form of proportional representation is ultimately the only fair way to represent the political wishes of the people. I also strongly applaud the Liberal Democrats' emphasis on the importance of education. I have no doubt that this ranks highest in all my priorities for government support. If we get our educational system in order and provide the best possible education, all else becomes so much easier and better. This is especially true for a future when, as automation increases, the meaning of employment changes, and where education is for life, not just for a particular job.

Sir Walter Bodmer was Professor of Genetics at Stanford and Oxford; he became Director of Research of the Imperial Cancer Research Fund in 1979, and Director-General for all the Fund's activities in 1991. In 1996 he retires from this position to become Principal of Hertford College, Oxford, but continues his active research into cancer, together with his wife, in Oxford.

PETER BOIZOT

The Liberal Democrats are the best party to fight for the freedom of the individual. This has been a great pillar of liberal and democratic philosophy since time began, and means one hell of a lot to me.

Our party stands the best chance of achieving individual liberty as it is not tied to the factions which control other parties and who by their very nature stifle them. The Liberal Democrats are the most likely to preserve freedom of the individual while at the same time creating a economically sound, caring and forward-looking society. Few political parties today look like breaking the shackles which modern life binds us with, but the Liberal approach offers the best hope to restore our freedom wherever possible.

Peter Boizot MBE founded Pizza Express Ltd in 1965 and has been chair of Pizza Express plc since 1993. He was a founder of the Soho Jazz Festival in 1986, and has been director of the Festival since then.

PROFESSOR BILL BRADSHAW

I have always felt uncomfortable with the certainties associated with authoritative points of view, whether political or religious. While some people need the comfort associated with the authority of evangelism or catholicism, or others have unfailing confidence in the invisible hand of the market or embrace the state as provider, I have always been uncomfortable with exclusive positions. Party discipline irks me because it crushes individualism and I believe that, like religious bigotry, it devalues the integrity of the individual. So for the whole of my life I have found the Liberal/Liberal Democrat party, however weak, as a place where individual opinion can be accommodated and where consensus is reached through discussion, genuine compromises and the acceptance that others, with a different view, have a valid point.

Because I genuinely want to work with people in other parties and with those who are apolitical I need to belong to a party which believes in a voting system which is likely to lead to governments of more than one party. Multi-party politics now works in much of local government and could be made to work nationally. Reform of the institutions of government to allow a more consensual approach to policy may be the big challenge of the next decade.

Bill Bradshaw has been a senior research fellow at the Centre for Socio-Legal Studies at Wolfson College, Oxford since 1985. He was General Manager of Western Region British Rail 1983–85 and Professor of Transport Management at Salford University 1986–92. He chaired the Party's policy working group on transport in 1994–95.

MALCOLM BRUCE MP

I am a Liberal Democrat because I believe, in spite of our traditions of fairness and tolerance, that the British political system is decadent, corrupt and in urgent need of radical reform which won't be brought about by the existing political establishment.

In a pluralist society every individual should be free to optimise their potential, subject only to the constraint of not inhibiting the freedom of others to do the same.

That requires every citizen to be given the basic opportunity to do this through access to decent education, health care and housing and the operation of a market economy reinforced by strong competition policy.

In particular, I believe the doctrine of a sovereign parliament has been used to centralise power under the political establishment. The rights of individual citizens can only be safeguarded by limiting the power of parliament through a Bill of Rights and the creation of a written federal constitution, sharing power with the nations and regions of the United Kingdom and the institutions of a more democratic European Union.

As a trading nation and former imperial power Britain needs a liberal and international outlook reinforced by unequivocal and positive, proactive support for the aims and ideals of the United Nations, the European Union and the GATT.

The divisions within the Tory Party and the lack of philosophical cohesion in New Labour leave me as convinced as ever that the only way the reforms needed for a genuinely vibrant pluralist society can be brought about is by winning a growing base of support for the Liberal Democrats.

Malcolm Bruce has been MP for Gordon since 1983; he joined the Liberals as a student at the age of 17, was a Liberal candidate in October 1974 and 1979, and is currently Treasury spokesman.

CLLR PAUL BURALL

The exhilaration of a good argument animated my schoolboy interest in politics. So, in 1959, I joined the Liberal Party. Why the Liberals? The smug self-satisfaction of Macmillan's Tories and the innate conservatism of Labour left no other choice for an enthusiast for change. That enthusiasm has survived the frustrations of supporting a party that has never, in my lifetime, held power nationally. In my early years, this loyalty probably had more to do with the people in the Party – from the heady inspiration of the 1960s Young Liberal leaders to the seductive charms of a particular Young Liberal Chair.

Over the years, my commitment has become more focused and my desire for change more compelling. My special interest is the environment and the potential catastrophes that we are creating with our continued abuse of the planet's recovery systems. In the past, our mistakes have been recoverable: by the time we understood the damage we were causing, there was still time to correct it before the results were too severe.

Now, the impact of our activities is so massive that mistakes may prove catastrophic before we have taken the necessary corrective action. The precautionary principle is therefore critical – yet it is rarely applied by politicians too scared to propose changes which might prove unpopular without absolute proof that the alternative is disaster.

That makes two of the basic tenets of the Liberal Democrats so important. The first is the Party's commitment to future generations, a commitment that leads it to put forward policies that may not be popular immediately but that are essential if humanity is to have a decent future. The second is its espousal of consensual rather than confrontational politics.

Sustainable economic, social and environmental policies demand continuity and courage and will never be achieved in a country riven by short term party points-scoring. The Liberal Democrat tradition of promoting consensus while taking risks in discussing new ideas is critical if British politics is to deliver a better future.

Paul Burall was Campaigns Director for the Design Council before becoming a freelance writer and lecturer specialising in design, environmental and business issues. He has been a county and district councillor and has chaired policy groups for the Liberal Democrats on subjects including planning, energy and environmental and economic sustainability.

DR ALAN BUTT PHILIP

Born into a politically aware household, it was the challenge of being refused a passport by the Home Office that brought me into politics. I joined the Liberal Party aged twelve, just before the first revival under Jo Grimond, and have stayed actively in the fold ever since.

The appeal of liberalism is manifold. It supports the individual's right to differ. It demands tolerance and fair play within society as a whole. It requires the application of reason to the conduct of politics. In Britain, liberalism has encouraged reform of our political and social institutions with an optimism that change is both possible and desirable. Above all, the liberty of the individual must be defended from the frequent and often arbitrary attacks of the state. Our country's history and experience should tell us that we should never assume that the institutions of a supposedly liberal democracy will always act in a liberal fashion. Hence the need for a Liberal Democrat party to guarantee the rights of the citizen and to remind our society to apply consistently the principles for which it thinks it stands.

The Liberal Democrats (and before them the Liberals) have long stood beyond the calls of vested interests, and for the upholding of certain values regardless of their unpopularity at given moments (eg the defence of the UK citizenship rights of Kenyan Asians or Hong Kong residents). The freedom that this gives the Party also enables it to challenge conventional wisdom, nowhere more consistently than in its support for European integration and constitutional and democratic reforms. I believe that the experience of participating in democratic decision-making at local levels – in schools, at work, in neighbourhoods – must be stimulated if democratic values are to remain well-rooted in our society.

Now the Liberal Democrats must give more emphasis to their environmental agenda and reinforce the necessity for our leaders and institutions to think long term. We also have to work harder to resolve the dilemma of having to solve major issues internationally without abandoning effective democratic control and local accountability.

Alan Butt Philip is Reader in European Integration at the University of Bath. President of the Oxford University Liberal Club 1965–66; parliamentary candidate for Wells 1973–87; fought Somerset in the 1979 Euro-election; Deputy Convenor, John Stuart Mill Institute.

JAMES CAMERON

I became a member of the Party relatively recently, transforming a vote into belonging. At my first conference I had something to do, made a speech, followed the progress of a policy proposal and felt like I had made a contribution. I felt some distance though. I am wary of mass opinion, I instinctively react against assumptions made about my beliefs, and in my professional life I am used to contesting arguments based on orthodoxies. Nonetheless, I found that I had at least two sets of argument for joining the Party.

Firstly, it is the party with the best policies for government now, and I am interested in making the best happen. This begins with priorities – education, constitutional reform and ecologically sustainable development – and ends with a collective state of mind about how to govern justly, with care and foresight.

Secondly, my convictions, part passionate, part intellectual, fit. They fit with others in the Party, with its history and its future. These convictions are centred on an idealism about the human spirit, the capacity of humans to do good and the moral purpose of government. That purpose may be to do less, better; it is always to use power delegated to it in order to move society towards its ideal, a generalised will to perfection – the creation of the good society. The status quo is never enough. Successful practical politics, it seems to me, is about the achievement of the better whilst pursuing the perfect. Knowing that you will fail to achieve that perfection, you must have the stamina, and humility, to keep progressing in small steps. I trust the Liberal Democrats to do that better than any other political party.

I support the focus on the individual, instinctive in the Party. If individual freedom and individual responsibility, formed in and by society from family to community, to state, to culture, are fundamental, then ultimately, care for the weakest members of our society is how we judge ourselves, the product of our own freedom. There are no borders to the vision of freedom from poverty, or the need to confront abuse of power or the desire to learn.

I like the slightly anarchic air to the Party, the disrespect for authority or orchestration, even the worthiness and decency that is so easy to ridicule. I like the curiosity in policy-making and the desire for openness in political institutions. Above all, I like the internationalist attitude of the Party. It is this which gives confidence that the Liberal Democrats will thrive amongst the world-transforming ideas in modern international society, from globalism to subsidiarity and sustainable development. In the medium term it provides the authority for leadership on the further development of Europe, a matter of profound significance for Britain.

James Cameron is a barrister and Director of the Foundation for International Environmental Law and Development (FIELD). In 1994–95, he chaired the Party's policy working group on international trade.

MENZIES CAMPBELL MP

My commitment to liberalism arises as much from instinct as reason. I do not claim any profound intellectual journey to a liberal position, it is rather that I never seriously or rigorously considered any alternative. As a fifteen year old schoolboy I instinctively disapproved of Suez, just when as a student I was appalled by British policy in Central Africa. Later, as a lawyer practising in Scotland, it was instinct which drove me to the conclusion that Home Rule was essential, and now it is instinct which persuades me that liberal values will best be preserved in a more united Europe and a better-managed United Nations.

In my active political life I have enjoyed the influence and friendship of Grimond, Steel and Jenkins. Whenever my instinct has been inadequate or insufficient their influence has been more than enough to keep me secure.

Menzies Campbell QC has been MP for North East Fife since 1987. He chaired the Scottish Liberal Party from 1975–77 and is currently Liberal Democrat spokesman on foreign affairs. From 1967–74 he held the UK 100 metres record.

DAVID CHIDGEY MP

Some people have to distance themselves from a situation before they can view it in perspective. Travelling from the United Kingdom to work at regular intervals regular intervals in places as diverse as Brazil and Bangladesh, Washington and West Africa, opened my horizons and then my mind to growing social injustice at home, fuelled by rampant Thatcherism.

To leave an office in Mayfair, and within 24 hours start living rough among village communities so deprived that they could only dream of a clean water supply, let alone health care, must be pretty high on the Richter scale of culture shocks. Long tropical nights free from social distraction, apart from a mountain of books one always meant to read, and the reassuring voice of the BBC World Service, provided the catalyst to appraise my goals and perspectives.

The Conservatives' general election victory under Margaret Thatcher in 1983 was the compelling motivation for me to defend the principles that life had shown to be paramount. Belief in every individual's right to develop their potential. Civilised society measured by individual freedom, hand in hand with social responsibility for the vulnerable, underpinned by a culture of investment in people's skills and the nation's infrastructure.

By now determined to make a contribution, however possible in the political arena, joining the Liberal Party was the obvious choice.

David Chidgey was a consulting engineer and international advisor to government agencies. He was elected MP for Eastleigh in the 1994 byelection; he previously fought Eastleigh in 1992, and Hampshire Central Euro-constituency in 1988 (byelection) and 1989.

TIM CLEMENT-JONES

Reasons for joining a party can be very different from those for adopting its philosophy. I joined the Liberal Party 22 years ago after working as a volunteer in the first years of existence of the North Kensington Neighbourhood Law Centre. It was the first of its kind, and it opened my eyes to the effects of Tory housing policy and the hardship and discrimination being suffered by so many people in post-Rachman Notting Hill. I has no knowledge of Liberal housing policies, and little of any of its other policies. My motives for joining were mainly reactive.

As a former Tory voter, all I knew was that Ted Heath had come in as right wing 'Selsdon man'. He had then done away with much of the protection given to private tenants. Subsequently he made a series of U-turns on a whole range of other policies. It was because he was so out of touch to begin with that he needed to change policies so dramatically, I reasoned. How, therefore, could Heath and his party be trusted over anything again? Why not choose a party that had been consistent in saying the same things it said in 1970 at the general election, and what's more was winning byelections! Joining Labour was out of the question because at that time I felt that trade unions were part of the problem, not the solution.

Initially I said that I would give five years to the Liberals and then reappraise. So much for that piece of self-delusion! Joining the Party – in

October 1973 – was a prelude to being sucked ever deeper into its processes and understanding more and more about its philosophy. For me the twin pillars became and have remained Community and Liberty. On the one hand, community politics – described in the Lishman/Greaves booklet *The Theory and Practice of Community Politics* of 1980 – and the spirit of devolution and 'trust in the people'; on the other a society which offers each individual the opportunity for self-fulfilment – 'life chances' so eloquently described in Ralf Dahrendorf's *New Liberty*, the text of his Reith lectures published in 1975.

Personalities often dominate the process of politics, which can be motivating but is not always an advantage – as I can can testify from experience of the Alliance! The best antidote is a strong underlying philosophy based on belief in a certain type of society, not simply a conviction about which party should be in power. That's why I am still an enthusiastic Liberal Democrat!

Tim Clement-Jones was Liberal Party Chair from 1986–88, during the merger process; campaign manager for Paddy Ashdown's leadership campaign and Chair of the 1994 Euro-election campaign; Chair, Federal Finance Committee since 1991; currently Deputy Chair, General Election Team; former company secretary and legal adviser of Kingfisher plc, now an independent corporate affairs consultant.

LORD DAHRENDORF

If one is active in public life, one needs a party. Being a cross-bencher may be a commendable state of mind, but it is not an effective way of taking part in debate. The party which comes closest to my beliefs and intentions is that of the Liberal Democrats. Why? Because I am a Liberal as well as a liberal.

The confession shifts the question to: why I am a Liberal. Because of a deep desire not to be fenced in, coupled with the sense that all others should enjoy freedom too. All constraints on our actions must be reduced to the minimum compatible with equal opportunities for all. This is why citizenship and life chances are central to my liberal creed: all citizens – in the final analysis, all humans: liberals are natural internationalists! – should have a large universe of choices open to them.

Liberals promote and defend the open society. We try and we err. Institutions are there to allow us to try again. The rule of law, democracy, competition in markets, rights of participation for all .... It all seems so simple, so obvious, and yet Liberals have to fight against enemies of the open society, of whom there are many. I am a Liberal also because I do not mind this fight.

Ralf Dahrendorf is Warden of St Antony's College, Oxford, and a Liberal Democrat peer. After an academic and political career in Germany he was European Commissioner, and Director of the London School of Economics 1974 –84.

JIM DALY

I have always been interested in organisations but at heart I am not an organisation man. I cannot abide corporate conformity, pretending to be loyal to convictions I do not share. The culture of organisational conformity stifles the expression of alternative ideas or even the voicing of reservation and doubt. In such an atmosphere, personal responsibility is absolved and it becomes easy to say 'I was only doing my job'. That was the lesson of the 1930s, but it needs constant reminders in every generation.

I got mine in 1979 when I found myself the vendor of a false prospectus as the Labour Party candidate for West London in the first election to the European Parliament. It was a bleak prospect and for me it seemed that political identity was lost.

But organisational conformity can be challenged. That happened for me when in November of that year Roy Jenkins gave the Dimbleby lecture, *Home Thoughts from Abroad.* He provided a rallying point and the vision for Britain as a modern parliamentary democracy.

The Liberal Democrats will do well to achieve the power to make it happen.

Jim Daly was Director of the Radical Centre, created to help Roy Jenkins in the period running up to the foundation of the SDP. He was Chair of the GLC Transport Committee and has kept up his interests in European Union affairs.

SIR GORONWY DANIEL

'We are what we are because we were what we were.' At least in my case, that statement helps to explain why I have long voted for the Liberals and recently agreed to be President of the Cardiff West local party of the Liberal Democrats.

My upbringing as a son of a mining engineer in the Welsh anthracite coalfield pointed me in that direction. He and my mother were Liberals and also devout chapel-goers. They insisted on Sunday School attendance and, after much effort, instilled in me a work ethic that got me to university in Aberystwyth where I graduated in geology in 1935. It was after early deviations to the right and then the left that I became convinced of the merits of a democratic centre party; and I was late in appreciating the full value of the Christian message.

My first deviation was in 1935 when I met Hitler Jügend in Germany's youth hostels. I was impressed by their new-found confidence in the future which was in sharp contrast to the unemployment and ineffective government in Britain. But my admiration was soon dissolved and I benefited from the decision I took to increase my qualifications for work by returning to Aberystwyth to take diplomas in three more subjects – anthropology, education and economic statistics. That work resulted in my acceptance by the Oxford Institute of Statistics to work for a doctorate on problems relating to the mobility of labour, and the award of a scholarship by Jesus College and a Fellowship by the University of Wales.

My second deviation took place during those years in Aberystwyth and Oxford when Marxism appeared to offer the best solution to the problems of the world, but events soon showed that to be a mistaken belief. Amongst the able people I had useful discussions with at the Institute was Harold Wilson, and it was he who introduced me to Valerie Lloyd George, to whom I have been happily married for 54 years.

The shortage of statisticians for the war effort resulted in my being called up to assist in the work of the House of Commons Select Committee on National Expenditure, and then to work in the new Ministry of Town and Country Planning. In 1947 I moved to the Ministry of Fuel and Power and in 1964 to be Permanent Secretary of the new Welsh Office. In 1969 I accepted the invitation to be Principal of the

University College in Aberystwyth and to take my turn as Vice Chancellor of the University of Wales. Whilst doing that work and subsequently I have been one of HM's County Lieutenants and, as Chairman, Deputy Chairman or member of many bodies I have been involved in different fields of work, including the Welsh language, television, the environment, banking and the theological college of the Welsh Independents.

Such experience as I have had (which also includes helping Sir Edward Heath in the European Commission negotiations) points to the value of the policies of the Liberal Democrats and their predecessors. It also shows the importance of those who, at material cost to themselves, work hard to ensure the Party's electoral success. That is why I do what I can to help them.

Sir Goronwy Daniel was Permanent Secretary at the Welsh Office, 1964–69, Principal of the University College of Wales at Aberystwyth, 1969–79 and Vice Chancellor of the University of Wales, 1977–79.

COLIN DARRACOTT

'*.... No-one shall be enslaved by poverty, ignorance or conformity ....*' This phrase encapsulates the Party's values.

In the months prior to the 1979 general election I was increasingly amazed to notice that Liberal Party politicians articulated my ideas and David Steel was developing my universal understandings of life and the universe into plausible policies for governance. With this arrogance, and notwithstanding the state of 'the poor old Liberal Party' at that time, I decided to contact the local Liberals to engage in the fun of the election campaign.

The local association provided me with new friends, fun and commitment. Six months later I was persuaded to join the Party. It was only then that I discovered the preamble to the constitution, and I felt like the ugly duckling in that frightful song, when he realises he is a swan. 'Good Heavens', I thought, 'I'm a Liberal!'

Understanding the balances between personal freedoms and collective responsibilities, and between community needs and global imperatives, is fundamental to Liberals in their formation of ideas and policy. Liberals understand the need for self-fulfillment, jointly and severally, and are like anarchists who compromise. That is why I see myself as a radical.

If I have contributed in return for the years of friendship, fellowship and motivation I have been given, it is the modest role in the 'greening' of the constitution's preamble which we moved at Assembly in the 1980s.

I didn't vote to decide to end the Liberal Party and form the Liberal Democrats, because I chaired the debate. The core values were being transferred to the Liberal Democrats, but although not an emotional person I must admit to feeling a strange mixture of glumness, relief and perplexity. What on earth was I doing presiding over this? How come I was shaking the hand of the man, David Steel, who had helped me realise I was a Liberal?

Colin Darracott joined the Liberal Party in 1979. Chair and President of London Liberal Party, Assembly/Conference Committee Chair, and member of various national committees. Oil trader and campaigner.

FRANCES DAVID

I was a member of the Labour Party. I trudged around my home town, Monmouth, with leaflets in favour of devolution in 1979, but Labour, which had introduced the referendum, let us down. When they sent me round Monmouth with leaflets for the European election I stopped to read them. I read that our Labour candidate for South East Wales did not want us to be in Europe at all. So I went home, threw the leaflets in the bin and had a cup of tea.

After that, I was a founder member of the SDP. It was marvellous. Policy could be discussed at every level and there was positive discrimination for women. David Owen was a serious problem for a CND supporter, of course, but we survived. He didn't.

The merger was much easier in Wales. Achieving it was traumatic but fun. And now the Party is going from strength to strength. I hope we will stick to our radical guns.

Frances David, a fomer deputy headteacher, is Deputy President of the Welsh Liberal Democrats. She fought the Monmouth byelection in 1991.

CHRIS DAVIES MP

What brought me into this party, and why do I feel comfortable with its beliefs? Looking back over the years I can think of quite a few formative points, but none of them was alone decisive.

My 12-year old outrage against the 'Beeching Axe' closure of many significant as well as many moribund railway lines has never left me. Anger is a great stimulant in politics. Thirty years later I usually only have to listen to a Tory Minister speaking on the *Today* programme to revive any flagging energies.

Environmental concerns became a paramount interest during my teens. Such religious beliefs as I hold are based principally on a sense of oneness with life on our planet in all its forms, and a certainty that mankind has the duty to strive to act as a caretaker, not as an asset stripper.

University years brought first the February 1974 election, and my moral support went to the Liberals for no better reason than that they were the underdog, albeit with the potential to be transformed into a Goliath-beating David. To see so many votes produce so few victories filled me with a sense of injustice, and that's still with me today whenever I consider Britain's moribund and rigged political institutions.

The October 1974 election followed soon after, and a Focus leaflet arrived through the door inviting me, indeed inviting anyone, to an election planning meeting in a neighbour's home. I went. It was my first experience of party political activity and I looked at the people there and thought, 'is this it? Surely I could do better than this'. By the time I'd cleaned the lavatories in the Liberal campaign HQ my tribal loyalties were well established.

But I might not have stayed had I not stumbled across some of the books written by Jo Grimond a decade before. His vision of modem liberalism, combining the desire of Lloyd George to use the power of the state for good with the principles of 19th century libertarian socialism, I discovered to be mine too.

I belong to this Party hook, line, and sinker. Although I may occasionally have disagreements, I feel comfortable with the Party's members. Confidence in my liberalism has over the years made me lazy when it comes to studying the Party's policy papers because I tend to assume I know what they will say.

Fortunately for my political career, I have usually been right.

Chris Davies was elected Liberal Democrat MP for Littleborough and Saddleworth in 1995, and is currently a spokesman on local government. He has been an activist since 1974, was Liverpool's housing chairman, 1982–83, and remains a councillor on Oldham MBC.

DR JENNY DAWE

Despite my maiden name being Beveridge, I was brought up in an apolitical, Tory-voting household which viewed my early and active involvement with the Liberals with incomprehension.

I joined the Scottish Liberal Party in the early 1960s while still at school. I had sent off for literature from all the political parties. But I found I had no choice. The policies and ideology of the Liberals were perfectly attuned to all I felt and believed in – and that remains so. People do and should always count. And, of course, I was full of admiration for Jo Grimond and John Bannerman.

Leaflet delivery, canvassing, designing quizzes which sold at sixpence a shot, debates, the Colne Valley byelection of 1963 (a hair-raising Scottish Young Liberal foray through the snow to a warm welcome from local farmers), being an election agent in a local ward and pulling the short straw to become Treasurer of Aberdeen University Liberals, are all memories of my early years in the Party.

Fourteen years in Tanzania and Malawi broke my membership but reinforced my belief that only Liberals had the morality and conviction to improve our world order.

On my return to Scotland I rejoined the Party, remaining a member ever since and fully endorsing our merger with the SDP in 1988. I have been as active politically as a busy academic and working life has allowed.

I have been a local council candidate, have proposed many successful motions at conference and have pounded the streets, banged on doors, climbed lampposts, sold jumble, designed leaflets, strung posters, and done all the other things which make being a political activist such hard work and good fun. Currently Edinburgh South local party Convenor and member of the Scottish Policy and Conference Committees, I have edited *Clifton Terrace Focus* – the Scottish Party's official gazette – since its inception in October 1993.

As a past Anti-Apartheid Movement member, founder signatory of Charter 88, member of the Scottish Council of Civil Liberties and of Amnesty International, it is probably no surprise that I put civil rights and liberties and constitutional reform high on my agenda of important issues.

I remain a Scottish Liberal Democrat because I believe in the empowerment and enfranchisement of individuals and in the creation of a fairer, freer, more open society. Only the Liberal Democrats are committed to the radical reform of the country's institutions which will enable these to happen.

My favourite poem is Hugh MacDiarmid's poignant *Little White Rose of Scotland:*

The Rose of all the world is not for me
I want for my part
Only the little white rose of Scotland
That smells sharp and sweet –
and breaks the heart.

For me, the Scottish Liberal Democrats are the little white rose of Scotland. Our policies are sharp, our ideology sweet, but, for now, my heart bleeds in anguish at our lack of political opportunity to make Scotland, Britain and the world a better and more compassionate place.

Dr Jenny Dawe was born and bred in Scotland; spent 14 years in Africa, has an African history PhD, is a welfare rights worker and has a family of four sons.

NAVNIT DHOLAKIA

Believe it or not but this is true.

I had left Tanzania at the age of seventeen. I chose to come to Britain for further studies. I ended up in Brighton. Why ?

Stuck on the noticeboard of the small railway station in a bush town in Tanzania was a map of Britain. No one could explain to me about the two projections on the south coast of this map until one day the District Commissioner came and explained that these were the famous Brighton piers. My knowledge of English was fairly limited. In the end a wise guy explained that these were the floating hotels. So I chose to come to the town of these floating hotels.

It was quite a culture shock to come to England in winter. At some stage I was invited by a friend to meet him in a pub on the seafront for a drink. I went there. There was a small group huddled in a corner. My friend was nowhere to be seen. Then a young man came to me. He explained that this was a meeting of the Young Liberals but they could not proceed because they were short of one person to form a quorum. I paid my half a crown and even now call myself a quorum Liberal.

This was a fruitful association. I became the Chairman of Brighton Young Liberals. This was the strongest Young Liberal movement in the country at that time. I then served as a parliamentary agent during the 1964 and 1966 general elections. Despite several promises of safe seats I have never wavered from my belief in the liberal values.

I value individual liberties. I will battle for individual rights. I abhor discrimination on the grounds of race, colour, national or ethnic origins. I value freedom and democracy. I am attracted towards a Bill of Rights. There ought to be a written constitution which would limit governmental powers and interference. Every citizen must have legal redress if their rights are infringed.

Liberal Democrats have been at the forefront of these issues. You have got to be a member of a minority group to realise how important these issues are.

Navnit Dholakia is a full time member of the Police Complaints Authority, and formerly Head of Administration of Justice Section at the Commission for Racial

Equality. He is a Vice Chairman of the National Association for the Care and Resettlement of Offenders and Chair of its Race Issues Advisory Committee.

PROFESSOR NORMAN DOMBEY

I saw Duncan Brack to discuss my piece for this collection on the day that the Dayton peace agreement on Bosnia was announced. To see why I am a Liberal Democrat is easy: just look at the different parties' approach to the Bosnian tragedy over the last three years. The Conservative Government's policy has at times been extraordinarily reminiscent of an earlier Conservative government's policy on Munich and Spain before World War II. Douglas Hurd never lost any opportunity to emphasise that the war in Bosnia was a civil war. But as Paddy Ashdown pointed out forcefully in the first full debate on Bosnia in the House of Commons (called by the Liberal Democrats) on 29 April 1993: 'I want to knock on the head the idea that has been perpetuated by the Foreign Secretary – and behind which he has taken cover to excuse matters – that this is a civil war. If it is, what on earth are we doing raising sanctions against Serbia and Belgrade? .... It is as logical to claim that this is a civil war as it is to claim that the events in Sudetenland in the 1930s were a civil war.'

At any suggestion of breaching the arms embargo on the Bosnians and Croats, who were the victims of Serbian aggression, there was general dismay from both Government and Labour spokesmen. Douglas Hurd spoke dismissively of a policy of, 'Here are the arms. Fight it out. That is the policy of the level killing field.' David Clark for Labour added his support: 'The Secretary of State is right when he says that we cannot lift the arms embargo to the Muslims. It has always seemed to us rather crazy to try to douse a fire with petrol. It never works.' As it turned out, it did work: the crucial element in the development of the Dayton peace was the US decision in November 1994 to stop enforcing the arms embargo against the Bosnian and Croatian governments. This decision made it possible for their armies to equip themselves, and subsequently led to the combined Croatian attack on Krajina, and the simultaneous Bosnian attack on Bihac of summer 1995 which so drastically changed the situation on the ground that the peace agreed at Dayton became possible.

Paddy Ashdown's speech in the Commons that day was remarkable in its vision and clarity; almost all of it was borne out by subsequent events. He dealt with the issue (or rather non-issue) of civil war; he emphasised that 'the truth is – it is a hard truth – that if we want to do anything effective, we cannot do it without troops on the ground. If we are not prepared to countenance that – and it seems that the Labour Party is not – we should not be in Bosnia at all.' That was a full two years before the setting up of the Anglo-French Rapid Reaction Force. Paddy carried on: 'We have acted throughout this crisis always too little and too late .... A terrible price has been paid by the innocents on the ground for that failure. Every attempt at peace .... has failed because the Serbs, and now the Croats, have always understood that they had more to gain from aggression on the ground than from the negotiating table .... Unless we were prepared to stop the aggression on the ground, there was no possibility that the Serbs would seriously negotiate.'

Paddy was also totally correct in his prediction of the impact of the events in Bosnia on the United Nations: 'the consistent year-long failure of judgement, leadership and action has led, as many of us predicted it would .... to the humiliation of the United Nations and the weakening of its international standing.' This was two years before the seizure by Mladic and his thugs of the UN-designated safe havens of Srebrenica and Zepa. Four years of UN failure has led to the total exclusion of the United Nations from the command structure of the international forces in Bosnia and to the return of NATO and the United States to a dominant position in European affairs. The United Nations has always played a pivotal role in Liberal Democrat views about world security, and we now have to come to terms with the new situation which has developed as a result of the events in Bosnia so clearly foreseen by Paddy Ashdown in April 1993.

Norman Dombey is Professor of Theoretical Physics at the University of Sussex. He has written on many areas of nuclear weapons/proliferation policy and has served on several Liberal Democrat working groups on security policy.

BERNARD DONOGHUE

Because I believe in justice and fairness.

Because I believe in equality and humanity.

Because I believe that an individual can make a difference.

Because I believe that a nation should serve its people.

Because I do not believe in the expedient or the short-term.

Because I believe that people are the most valuable resource.

Because I believe that poverty cannot be tolerated.

Because I believe that bigotry and prejudice weaken and diminish us

Because I believe that the only vested interests in politics should be one's beliefs.

Because I believe that we have obligations and responsibilities to each other.

Because I believe in passion and principle rather than dogma or dictat.

Because I believe that there is such a thing as society.

Bernard Donoghue is Chairperson: Disability Daily Consortium; Association of Combined Youth Clubs; London Youth Matters; British Youth Council; the Party's policy working groups on disability and youth policies. Campaigner and parliamentary adviser.

ANDREW DUFF

European unity and world order

The Paris *événements* of May 1968, and the exciting possibilities there opening up, shaped my politics. Brought up partly in a decaying Birkenhead and partly in a reactionary public school (Sherborne), I was ripe for liberation. The causes of Reform and Europe met up, and set me to try to articulate a politics that will make Britain a modem European place and will make a united Europe a force for peace and prosperity in the world.

Although I was much influenced by Roy Jenkins, Shirley Williams, George Thomson and Dick Taveme, I left Labour to join the Liberals in 1974. This was a bit of a homecoming: in the 1920s my family had owned the only motorcar in the Birkenhead Liberals. My first employer, nevertheless, was the late, great Labour MP John Mackintosh – the veritable precursor of the SDP, whose emergence I (then a Cambridge councillor) strongly supported.

The eventual frustration of the Alliance reinforced my view that it was not possible to reform the UK on our own resources. Political thought and means of action had to be imported from the mainland; and the European Community, that radical success for liberalism, had to be used by the British with skill and bold imagination. The ties that now bind me to the Liberal Democrats have not changed. Federal European union is the way to modernise Britain, to assert popular sovereignty and to ensure justice and fair play. European unity, currency reform and Scottish Home Rule are the great liberal causes of this decade.

Andrew Duff is Chair of the English Liberal Democrats and Director of the Federal Trust.

ADMIRAL SIR JAMES EBERLE

For my 43 years in the Royal Navy, I was, as was appropriate, non-political in a party sense. But I generally voted Conservative. Subsequently as head of the independent institute, the Royal Institute of International Affairs, I knew well Denis Healy's second law of politics – he that stands in the middle of the road gets hit by the traffic going in both directions. Nevertheless, the experience of 50 years brought me to the view that the effectively 'bipolar' nature of British politics had not served the UK well. I became a floating voter. (What else would you expect an Admiral to be?!)

During the lead-up to the Gulf War, Paddy Ashdown asked me to join a small informal advisory group on the military/political aspects of the campaign. Subsequently, I was asked to advise on aspects of the Party's defence and security policy – and subsequently to speak on such matters during the election campaign. Gradually, I became more involved at the interface between international politics, about which I had considerable experience, and domestic politics, about which I knew all too little. Later, I found myself giving advice on defence policy issues at a high level Party policy committee meeting, and realised that I had better become a proper paid up member of the Party! Later still, I found myself increasingly involved in countryside issues, issues that were generally much better understood among Liberals than in the Conservative or Labour Parties.

British politics have, in my view, entered a very dangerous phase. Intolerance and 'political correctness', linked and dangerous tendencies, are creeping increasingly into our daily lives. Our society is becoming increasingly litigious. The violence of some single interest pressure groups are moving us towards a state of incipient anarchy. The principles of my liberal and democratic beliefs, the freedom of the individual to make his own choices, the responsibility of the individual for him or herself, the importance of the family, the protection of the rights of minorities, and a movement towards cooperational rather than confrontational politics , are important for me. I find them principally under the Lib Dem banner. What other choice could I make? It is a choice I have never regretted.

Admiral Sir James Eberle was a member of the Board of Admiralty and Commander in Chief UK Fleet; from 1984–91 he was Director of the Royal Institute of International Affairs.

PAUL EKINS

At the end of the twentieth century, humanity is beset with many challenges and problems. This is not a new situation; nor are many of the problems new, though, of course, their modern manifestations may be particular to the age: war, poverty, unemployment, disregard for human rights or democratic principles – none of these blots on human society are peculiar to the modern world. Clearly one expects a political party to have clear positions with regard to these issues. The Liberal Democrats do, and they are positions with which I broadly agree. But that is not why I am a member.

In addition to the above intransigent political problems, there is another which is quite specific to our age, a problem the resolution, or otherwise, of which will have more long-lasting and profound implications for humanity as a whole than any other with which political parties, or anyone else, are currently engaged. The issue is the unprecedented destruction by humanity of the earth's living systems and the global changes to the biosphere that such destruction is already bringing about.

This issue represents a political challenge of appalling difficulty and complexity. The changes are very slow, over long timescales, but are very difficult if not impossible to reverse, often requiring settled policy over decades. Political timescales, on the other hand, are short, and susceptible to the whims of public opinion, while political cut and thrust thrives on adversarial opposition rather than a measured consensus for the benefit of future generations.

Moreover, some aspects of the issue challenge some of the most settled expectations of the industrial consumer society, such as the enjoyment of high levels of mobility based on near-universal ownership of the private motor car, or an annual, indefinite increase in private and social consumption. Challenging such expectations remains a dangerous, if not suicidal, course of action for any political party.

Just as difficult to address, if different, is the interaction between environmental issues and those of economic development as they relate to less or non-industrialised countries. The huge disparities between and within countries, and the enormous current populations of the developing world that are seeking to join the global consumer society, not to mention the even larger populations that are in prospect, make the achievement of environmental sustainability a political task of giant dimensions.

The Liberal Democrats have not yet got a fully worked out programme to address these issues. But they acknowledge clearly, consistently and on a par with other issues that the environment is an issue that must be addressed and addressed now. They do not shrink from some of the more difficult policy positions that are prerequisites of sustainable development, such as a carbon tax, reform of the rules of world trade or a shift in transport priorities away from the private car to public transport, cycling and walking. In their policy positions at the national level, and in the actions of their councils at the local level, the Liberal Democrats are showing themselves to be the only major UK party that is fully aware of the environmental challenge and is determined to lead the British public on this issue rather than be buffeted about by it.

Such leadership is politically risky for as long as the wider electorate remains ignorant, apathetic or defeatist with regard to environmental issues. Yet such leadership is essential to help overcome these obstacles to sustainability. That is why support for the Liberal Democrats at this time is an important statement of environmental commitment. For me that is the most important commitment that it is possible to make.

Paul Ekins is a senior lecturer at the Environmental Policy Unit at Keele University and a Director of Forum for the Future. *He has served on Party policy working groups on economics, employment, sustainability and international trade.*

LYNNE FEATHERSTONE

The Power of One

It took me twenty years to commit to a political party. I proudly marched against 'Maggie Thatcher – union snatcher' in student days in the early '70s, when to be anything other than revolutionary would have ruined one's social life. And then realised when Labour finally did come to power the grim reality of their government. Thus believing both the Tories and Labour to be fatally flawed and regarding the Liberals, politically speaking, as non-starters, I turned my back on politics and concentrated on real life. Twenty years on, as I watched society falling into the abyss, I realised that the political process *is* real life and if I wanted a different reality I would have to fight for it within that process.

Looking deeply into the political pot to see where my energies could best be targeted, I found that what once in its raw 'Liberal' form appeared to be simply a rather woolly view of individualism had now grown up and become a well-rounded political ideology. Liberal Democracy now provided the political hook on which to hang my hat. Not perfect – no system is – but in the end political expression must externalise personal core belief; and for me that is, and has always been, fairness and the power of one. The power of one is the most potent force for change which exists on this planet.

– 'THE POWER OF ONE' IS THE TITLE OF A BOOK BY BRYCE COURTNAY.

Lynne Featherstone is Vice Chair of Women Liberal Democrats and PPC for Hornsey & Wood Green. She is a strategic design consultant and writer.

CLLR SUSAN FENWICK

The first election I remember taking an interest in was in 1974, when I asked my grandmother who she wanted to win and why. 'The Conservatives, of course.' The why was more difficult. 'Because I've always been a Conservative'. She was my first example of the working class Tory.

I then received my first lesson in the British electoral system. Could someone please explain to me why Mr Wilson was going to be Prime Minister when more people had voted for Mr Heath? My mother did as best she could, explaining first past the post and coalition politics to a 12 year-old. I was not impressed. 'But that isn't what people voted for,' I cried. Twenty years later, not much has changed.

However, politics was about to change my life forever. For the past year or so I had been told about this important test I would sit in my last year of primary school. Then one day I was told that I didn't have to take it any more. I thought this was great news, but my mother thought it was disastrous. I remember her writing letters to everyone under the sun protesting about 'comprehensive education'. She worked on the principle that the more letters a politician received on the subject the more likely they were to listen (a lesson I now understand as a councillor). So I had written, my grandmother had written, I think she even wrote as my eight year old brother. I remember her telling my great-uncle that he had written to the Education Secretary to protest, something he was not unreasonably upset about given he had not been asked and was a lifelong socialist! I often heard interesting but rather sterile debates between these two. This helped me turn off traditional Labour/Tory politics.

Despite the best intentions of my mother, comprehensive education was introduced and I was sent to private school. The next six years of privileged education, Tory parents and a Labour government had a big influence on my political philosophy. Then I grew up. I often think that Tories are people who have never really grown up.

Crunch time happened. The 1983 general election and my first vote loomed. I decided that I wanted to make a difference and break the stranglehold of Tory/Labour politics. I voted Alliance.

I never do things by half. Having voted I wanted to join, change the system and breathe some life back into politics (I was only 21!).

I could put forward many philosophies that are important to me, which will no doubt be put more eloquently by others. But as I watch the Labour Party shamelessly ditching everything they are supposed to stand for I am reminded what is crucial to me. I am a liberal because honesty is fundamental to me. I don't mean that everyone should live their lives without ever being untruthful, but on the big things, the issues that matter, like how you are going to run the country, you have to be honest and you have to have trust. That is unfortunately what politics has lost, largely because of the antics of the Labour and Tory parties. I hope it is something we always hang on to.

Susan Fenwick jumped over the border to escape Scottish socialism and is now a councillor in Richmond upon Thames. She works in housing, is doing a MBA at Warwick and chairs the Party's housing policy group. Occasional time off is spent on the golf course, or sampling the contents of a bottle of good wine.

PADDY FITZGERALD

For very many years I remained an uncommitted voter. I cast my vote for the party that most reflected my analysis of the country's need at the time.

During those early years, the Liberal Party appeared to me as a fringe party. Later I had concerns over the turbulence occasioned by the mergers and schisms that took place.

But the choice of where to cast my vote was becoming an increasing problem; Labour seemed in thrall to unions and left, Conservatives were moving from the early years of Thatcherism to the unacceptable face of a dogma pursued to an illogical conclusion. I faced the choice of competing ideologies, neither satisfactory.

How could the country get into a situation where both the viable alternatives were so unappealing to so many? In Brussels a senior executive said: 'I do not understand the British; you have two representatives and they invariably vote against each other. Every other country recognises the importance of making their votes count'. From any point of view confrontational politics was clearly not the answer, and proportional representation seemed increasingly attractive.

Liberal Democrats were the only advocates of PR, and this led me to take a much longer and harder look at the Party.

In the short term there might be little chance of a Liberal Democrat government, but their position had other attractions. For success the Party would have to be the party of change, would have to embrace innovation and would in essence be the goad within parliament. Voters would choose Liberal Democrats because of their new and vibrant solutions to the challenges and opportunities facing us; if the Party not only had new ideas that attracted voters but continued to innovate .... that intellectual leadership would ultimately be reflected in the ballot box.

Becoming a Liberal Democrats represented a much deeper level of commitment. It appealed because there were areas where I felt I could contribute to the process, and because to me membership of a party was only justified through involvement.

In my past work I had been required to develop strategies which combined short term pragmatism with long term objectives. So I wanted to contribute, I felt I had skills of use, and I believed the Party could use these in its generation of policy.

But the clincher related to values. These seemed based on neither envy nor exploitation, but on creating a society that the vast majority of its members could be proud of and enjoy. A party that could produce a vision for a step change out of continuing decline.

That's why I joined up.

Paddy FitzGerald is a member of the Party's policy working group on higher education. and is a consultant in education and health (Partners in Care). She was formerly Academic Director of the European Business School and Dean of Brighton Business School.

JONATHAN FRYER

I grew up in a Labour rotten borough, living in a rotten Tory household. So I suppose I was predestined to gravitate towards the Liberals. But it was Jo Grimond who clinched it. He came to speak to my school in 1964, presumably as part of the general election campaign. Fourteen and bare-kneed, I couldn't vote. But I sat there transfixed thinking: 'Hang on, that's what I believe!'

Comfortingly, that's what I have continued to feel for most of the intervening three decades. No political party could ever be perfect. Yet I have been repeatedly delighted to find that when a new situation arose, the Party – in its various transmogrifications – produced a line very much in harmony with views I had arrived at independently.

Internationalism has always been a crucial factor in my allegiance. Not just the deep commitment to the evolution of the European Union in the interest of all its citizens, but also a genuine awareness of Britain's role in furthering equitable and sustainable global development.

Like so many other Party stalwarts, I have done my stints on the hustings, national and European, without ever tasting the elixir of power (though I did serve a term as a London borough councillor). One learns to savour success vicariously, cheering others on at byelections, or sitting up late at night, glued to the *Newsnight* election special.

Then there is the friendship that makes Party conferences and regional gatherings as much social as political events. I believe we shouldn't be afraid of treasuring that. After all, after so many years in the blue chill of Tory Britain, it's reassuring to be able to huddle together in a golden glow.

Jonathan Fryer is a writer, lecturer and broadcaster, and Honorary Consul of Mauritania in the UK.

TUDOR GATES

I think it was about 1958, sharing a platform in Bethnal Green with Jo Grimond, that I blurted out an impromptu definition of Liberals as compared with Labour and Conservative supporters. I said we were socialists without dogma, or Tories with a conscience. Almost forty years later, I haven't changed my mind much.

I wanted the brave new postwar world as much as anyone else. A child of the thirties, I felt a bitterness (which I have never lost) towards the Tories for those bleak years, and was glad to see them go.

Attlee and that Labour government of giants (Bevan, Bevin, Cripps, Morrison et al) did a great job of implementing the Liberal Sir William Beveridge's report. If only they had not gone over the top, trying to realise Clause 4 – dogma, you see – which put them in the clutch of the unions. In the fifties and sixties, the political seesaw went up and down. Liberals glimpsed (but never much more) a sight of the promised land. All we could really do was keep the flag flying, make sure we were at least in the race. Which is how the British electorate saw its general elections, as a two-horse race. You could only back one or the other of the front-runners. The Liberals also ran.

Then came the seventies, inflation out of control, a brief flirtation with power during the Lib-Lab Pact, and the final crunching confrontation with the unions in that winter of discontent with its inevitable tragic aftermath, sixteen years of uninterrupted Tory rule.

Why, oh why, did it have to happen? Did Labour and the trade unions have a suicide pact? I had always belonged to a trade union (one had to) but it was about 1970 that I became an activist, on much the same grounds as I became a politician, namely that this was too serious a business to be left to the professionals.

Maggie Thatcher brought in some much-needed trade union reform, which Liberals – now part of the Alliance – by and large supported, and still do. She was not magnanimous in victory, however, and, having brought the miners to their knees, did not hesitate to put in the boot, introducing legislation which was no longer corrective but punitive, even malevolent. (That still continues, by the way.) Yet the trade union movement, for all its errors, is probably the body most responsible for there being a system of social justice in this country; the fall of the former and the weakness of the latter at this time is no coincidence.

Why on earth did I become a Liberal when I could have pursued exactly the same paths but under a flag of convenience, when in recompense for my labours I would now be a peer of the realm? What is it about faith in a cause that makes one so doggedly court failure – again and again? Perhaps it's playing the game, not winning, that's important. Perhaps electoral failure is the failure of the electorate, rather than the elected. Whatever the reason, I still go on. I still believe.

Why am I a Liberal? Is it because at heart I'm an eternal compromiser, always seeking the middle path? And if so, is that so bad? Why cannot entrepreneurial spirit be encouraged without resorting at the same time to sickening greed? Why, in banding the workers of this country together in order to protect their interests, is it necessary to seek to dictate to government?

Why am I a Liberal? Because I am a social democrat but I have no time for dogma. Because I believe in free enterprise but I still have, and always will, a social conscience.

Plus que ça change ....

Tudor Gates is a playwright, novelist, screenwriter, film producer and trade unionist. He is the President, Association of Liberal Democrat Trade Unionists; former President, ACTT; former Joint President, BECTU. Six times parliamentary candidate.

MICHAEL GERMAN

It would be easy to say that my entry into the Liberal Party was a result of a burning desire to deal with injustice, accelerate freedoms and develop my empathy with oppressed minorities. The truth is, that the Liberal Party enhanced my feel-good factor with society to a point where it triggered my application for membership. I was inspired by the humanity of Jo Grimond.

The glue holding me to party is of the super variety rather than that of the Pritt Stick much loved of pre-personal computer Focus editors. My optimism for Liberal values has been much buffeted. Amazingly it has remained firm despite my closeness to the party alliance, splits, schisms, and merger of the 1980s, and to the trauma of seeing the Liberal candidate in next door Cardiff South in 1979 tear up his papers two minutes before close of nomination, declaring for the Tories against the incumbent Jim Callaghan.

So why do I stay? In essence because the Liberal Democrats alone offer an equilibrium between Liberty, Equality, and, most crucially, Community.

Michael German was a parliamentary candidate in Cardiff in 1974, 1979, 1983 and 1987, Leader of the Liberal Democrat Group, Cardiff City Council 1983–96, and has been a member of various Party Committees including the Federal Policy Committee and Federal Executive. He was the Welsh Party's General Election Campaign Director in 1992, and will be again in the forthcoming election.

ZERBANOO GIFFORD

1892 saw the election of Dadabhai Naoroji, the first, and so far last, non-white Liberal to sit in parliament. Almost forgotten in Britain, he is still adored by millions as the Grand Old Man of India.

In numerous ways, Naoroji was more radical than the other politicians of his day. He championed causes such as equality for women, supported moves to improve working people's lives, and fought against the economic exploitation of poorer countries by the richer. His example inspired me to join the Liberal Party many moons ago.

It was difficult for Naoroji to be selected in a winnable seat then, but you would imagine that, a century on, the Liberal Democrats would realise the benefits of having representatives of the ethnic minority communities in parliament, especially since Britain is now a multi-cultural society.

The Party's constitution starts off with fine words about welcoming this diversity and opportunity. Party policy recognises that many of the problems of Naoroji's time remain with us today. Britain still suffers from racial discrimination and the under-representation of women and minorities.

Yet if Naoroji were around today, he'd stand little chance of being a Liberal Democrat MP. Aged 66 when elected, selection panels would tell him he was far too old. Born in India, he would be 'unrepresentative' of the area, so perhaps he might try Southall? His concern for people outside the constituency, never mind overseas, would count against him in today's obsession to have a 'local' candidate. About the only point in his favour would be being a professional middle-class man.

Today, I fear that Dadabhai Naoroji would not join the Liberal Democrats. The Party is not radical enough for someone of his dynamic and inclusive vision. Another party is leading the way to increase parliamentary representation for women and the minorities. That would sadden him, I'm sure, as it saddens me.

Zerbanoo Gifford is an author, Director of Anti-Slavery International, a former Liberal councillor, parliamentary candidate and Chair of the Party's Community Relations Panel. Holder, Nehru Centenary Award.

PHILIP GOLDENBERG

I am a liberal by values because I believe in tolerance, open-mindedness and generosity of spirit (the last being the meaning of the Latin word *liberalis*).

I am a Liberal Democrat for three reasons.

Firstly, the Party reflects and gives voice to my values. It is founded on human rights, and believes that institutions only have value insofar as they serve the people they represent.

Secondly, the Party's analysis of the current political situation – both domestically and internationally – is fundamentally and distinctively right. The policies it propounds – founded on a combination of economic realism, social cohesion, participation and empowerment – are both apt and honest, and often imaginative and far-sighted, with a holistic approach, particularly on environmental issues.

Thirdly, the Party is in many ways my – somewhat extended! – family. It attracts people who, while gloriously different as individuals, share a common set of values, a similar mindset and a notable collective sense of humour, with that self-deprecating strand which is often the hallmark of minority groups.

Philip Goldenberg has fought five Westminster elections, and narrowly missed election to the European Parliament in 1994. He was a local councillor for eight years, and has been heavily involved in the formulation of Party policy. He advised the former Liberal Party on its merger with the former SDP, and was co-author of the original constitution of the Liberal Democrats.

SIR WILLIAM GOODHART QC

Let me start with a paradox. I am a passionate believer in scepticism. Constructive scepticism, that is – something very different from cynicism. I believe in tolerance, diversity, pragmatism. I hate all forms of fundamentalism – religious, political or nationalistic. I distrust theories which claim to provide answers to political, economic or social problems. Some of them (Adam Smith and Keynes) help to explain and improve our systems; but others (Marx) are huge disasters.

All this could be said across a pretty wide spectrum of British politics. Why then am I specifically a Liberal Democrat? Because I believe that the role of government is not just to preserve law and order but is to help to build a civilised and tolerant society. Ordinary people must be protected from oppression by monopolistic business, by over-mighty trade unions, by public authorities, sometimes (as in Northern Ireland) by other ordinary people. People must be given opportunities through education, and protected from disease and want through public health services and social security. Yet government must know its own limitations. The economy is not a machine but a kind of living organism; governments can try to guide it but can never successfully direct it.

I am a Liberal Democrat because I believe that we, more than any other party, recognise both the responsibilities and the limitations of government. Democracy has been described as the least worst political system. We, I believe, are the least worst political party. From a sceptic, that is high praise.

Sir William Goodhart QC, a barrister, helped write the SDP and Liberal Democrat constitutions and has been Chair of both Parties' Conference Committees. He has been a member of the council of Justice since 1972 (Chair, 1988-94).

LINDSAY GRANSHAW

It took American Marxists to show me that I was a social democrat in the European tradition.

I went to the United States as a PhD student in 1976, to a department where I was surrounded by left-wingers. Most of my fellow students were 'mature', many had been anti-Vietnam war protesters and several had fought in Vietnam; they had come to study, critique and undermine the military-industrial complex which they identified as the major factor in the origin and continuation of that war. Their passion, commitment and intellectual rigour were impressive. They were not playing politics – their experience had driven them to activism. Most were various shades of Marxist, quite different from younger American students, whose energy was largely devoted to securing lucrative places in medicine, law or business. Quite different, too, from my Oxford undergraduate contemporaries, whose only activism had consisted of occupying the exam halls to demand a students' union.

But though these Marxists impressed me, I could not accept their ultimate submergence of individual rights within those of the group. My more liberal and social democratic views crystallised, and I decided that when I returned to Britain, I had to become actively involved in politics.

I arrived back just before the SDP was launched in the spring of 1981, and I joined immediately. It seemed to me that the SDP resolved in all key areas that old tension between the needs of the individual – liberty – with social justice. The SDP's promotion of women in politics acted as a further challenge. No sooner had I attended a first meeting than I was organising a ward, standing as a council candidate and then for parliament. I soon came to find politics thoroughly absorbing, usually a lot of fun, though sometimes quite awful. I never doubted that Britain needed what the SDP in alliance with the Liberals was putting forward.

After the 1987 election I joined the Liberal Democrats, as the successor to the SDP. I had seen the two parties work well together locally, and was one of the team who negotiated merger. I was not prepared for the messiness and distrust between the two parties nationally, with prejudices persisting even now, but I remain convinced that merger was the only way forward.

So here I am, more battered and bruised than I was in 1981, but perhaps having learned something on the way. For me, the Party's commitment to the long term – its emphasis on education and political reform – is vital. And I do not have to look far to see that it is still the Liberal Democrats who best resolve the balance between the individual and social justice.

Lindsay Granshaw was Chair of Women Liberal Democrats. Formerly a university lecturer, she divides her time between children, politics and writing.

BERNARD GREAVES

I discovered liberalism in 1960 by reading Lord Acton. His master work, *The History of Liberty,* was never written, but his notes for it, held in the university library at Cambridge, make clear what would have been its central themes:

that liberty is the end product of politics and not its starting point;

that the central political issue is the structure of the institutions through which power is exercised;

that power should be dispersed, because when concentrated it becomes dangerous and liberty is put in jeopardy;

that federalism is the means of achieving that dispersal, is capable of limitless extension in both the horizontal and vertical dimensions, and that its structures need be neither static nor rigid but can be dynamic and changing;

that progress towards liberty, despite inevitable setbacks, is developmental such that any individual, generation or society builds on the experience and achievements of those that have gone before.

Thus my liberalism has a firm philosophical foundation that is rational, radical and moral; the route by which I found it was difficult and personal.

In the summer of 1958, approaching the age of 16, I realised I was in love with another boy. Without understanding it, I had been in love with Mike for over two years. Painfully over the succeeding years I established for myself a gay identity, in a world in which as yet there was no gay community nor sub-culture, where little was written and even less spoken of a subject still largely taboo, and in which even the word itself was not in currency.

I felt betrayed. If those who had brought me up could so mislead me, and so devalue feelings that lay at the core of my being, I could no longer take on trust anything they said. Henceforth I would rely on my intellect and the quality of my experience to form my own judgements.

My abandonments of the conservative and Christian ethos that surrounded me soon brought me into conflict with the hierarchical structures of my public school. I went up to Cambridge University in 1961 feeling emotionally, intellectually and politically alone, with Lord Acton as my sole mentor. To my surprise I met there a group of people who thought the same way that I did. They were all Liberals.

By 1971 I was just beginning to establish myself at a national level within the Liberal Party. That summer, driven by a controlled anger, I exposed the outrageous methods being used by the police to entrap gay men in public toilets in Cambridge. I was right in expecting that everyone would assume I was gay. I was wrong in expecting it would end my career in the Liberal Party. Within six years I was a national officer; and in 1979 we became the first political party in the UK to fight a general election with an unequivocal manifesto commitment to legal equality for gay people. I was proud to be a Liberal.

Just one hundred years ago, in 1895, my great-grandfather stood for parliament as a Liberal. Adam Lee was Mayor of Oldham and, like his contemporary Lord Acton, both an advocate of Irish Home Rule and an adviser to Gladstone. Perhaps they even knew one another. Maybe my liberalism owes less to my personal experience and more to that family tradition than I care to acknowledge.

Bernard Greaves is a former Publicity Officer and Director of Policy Promotion for the Liberal Party; joint author, The Theory and Practice of Community Politics *(1980); Treasurer, Leicester West Liberal Democrats; member, crime & policing policy working group and equal opportunities audit group.*

CLLR TONY GREAVES

Why I am (possibly) a Liberal Democrat

Fundamentally I am not a 'Liberal Democrat' for fundamentally I don't know what it means!

Only very rarely is a new political ideology invented. Liberal democracy is a set of ideas underlying kinds of government, but it is not an ideology and nothing has happened in the past eight years to turn it into one.

But simply in order to survive, the Liberal Democrats need an ideology. Liberalism needs a party. And as a liberal who wishes to take an active and serious part in politics, I too need a party. There is really only one choice on offer.

At the end of the last century a myriad forms of socialism were blossoming as 'new' ideologies. A hundred years on they are all wilting. People in the future may see socialism as the great heresy of the 20th century. So perhaps liberalism now has its chance?

But why such an unfashionable thing as ideology?

Politics is about the relationship of people to each other within the totality of humankind, and about their relationship with their environment. It is about people. That is inevitable since we are people and none of us can view anything at all except as people. We may wish we were gods or frogs or cybermen but we are not.

Ideologies are simply different views of the way people should relate to each other within society; different sets of principles on which to base political action.

This is so even for proponents of the latest ideology – an extreme 'green' view of the world. They are simply redefining the position and role of people in relation to the whole ecological system and therefore to each other.

Some ideologies are essentially authoritarian, some egalitarian; some based on religious beliefs, others on rationalism. Some are centred upon the primacy of leaders, national or other groups, class or gender or position.

Liberalism is fundamentally libertarian, tolerant and generous. It starts with people as individuals, with equal fundamental rights and the equal right to regard by others, not with categories or groups, whether inherited, imposed or chosen. It emphasises the equal inherent value and importance of each one and seeks ways in which they can enjoy the freedom to develop their talents and their lives to the full.

In order to fulfil their potential, people have to live in society and relate to each other. Relationships between people should therefore be based on openness, consent and voluntary involvement; not on decisions made by elites in secret and imposed by authority, whether arbitrary or according to rules laid down from on high, or even imposed by a majority if they deny basic individual rights.

It means tolerance in personal relationships; economic and political systems based on democracy; and freedom in all spheres, personal, social and economic, to the maximum extent that it does not impose unreasonably upon others.

Perhaps we can dream that, with the end of socialism, liberalism may flourish in the 21st century as the genuine libertarian left, in active opposition to all the malignant forces of corporatism and the greedy and intolerant right which are growing in strength throughout the world?

So I do my best to encourage the Liberal Democrats to become truly liberal, and liberals to truly embrace the Party. And I produce Focus leaflets and try to help create a liberal local community. What else can I do?

Tony Greaves is a councillor on Lancashire County Council and Pendle Borough Council, and a dealer in out-of-print political bookers and pamphlets.

GWYN GRIFFITHS

Although I strongly supported the actions of the Heath Government in taking Britain into Europe, the longer term consistency and virtual unanimity of Liberal support for membership was probably the decisive factor in leading me to join the Welsh Liberal Party in October 1974. The referendum the following year was the first time that I was extensively involved in a campaign, and it was probably the success of that experience of members of different parties working together towards a common goal that has affected my attitude ever since.

Having repeated the exercise in the 1979 devolution referendum and again in the course of cooperation with the SDP, I find the virulent and often personal attacks on political opponents to be the most depressing thing about British politics. They have often made me less enthusiastic than I would otherwise have been about both conference speeches and some election campaigns.

Although it was Europe that brought me into the Liberal fold, I rapidly became conscious that it was the attachment to civil liberties, human rights and constitutional reform which made me a liberal. Like many others, it was the preamble to the Liberal Party constitution that best encapsulated for me the the values which we share.

I have become increasingly convinced that those values can only be protected by wholesale constitutional reform. In particular the elected dictatorship of Westminster government must be broken down by the decentralisation of power to the nations and regions of the UK, as well as the sharing of sovereignty with our European colleagues.

Although I continue to be very happy to work with others towards common goals it is only the Liberal Party, and now the Liberal Democrats, that have shown strong and consistent commitment to both these processes and that is why it remains the only party for me.

Gwyn Griffiths a solicitor, a member of the Welsh Language Board and the Council for the Preservation of Rural Wales, and constitutional adviser to the Welsh Liberal Democrats.

PROFESSOR BRIAN GROOMBRIDGE

For most of my life there has been a close, deepening relationship between politics and education. My school, Midhurst Grammar, awakened an interest in politics around 1940. Democracy was not only on the curriculum there. It informed the way the school was run. I chaired my first meeting when I was 14. Later I chose to work in adult education, a decision at the time regarded as odd, almost like dropping out, but for me it made political as well as personal sense. There was model value in the concept of a negotiated curriculum, with students and tutors learning from one another, both often motivated by a desire to improve society as well as enabling individuals to grow. I had a major spell in educational broadcasting, and served on the democratically visionary Planning Committee of the Open University, through which knowledge could be shared on a socially significant scale. Ever since 1951, my work has benefited from international cooperation (mutual learning again), through channels such as UNESCO, the European Broadcasting Union and the European Bureau of Adult Education.

With this background, I became increasingly interested in politics, though not in party politics. I conscientiously voted anti-Tory in whatever was the most effective way available, but my work stayed relevant to education for democratic citizenship. Like many others, I am now concerned for the health and future of democracy itself. When it comes to democracy, Britain is no longer a world leader. Extraordinary to remember that the word means 'people power'. Before the second world war, Britain was an oligarchy, redeemed by certain democratic assumptions and procedure. Then, despite the 'welfare state', the democratic project itself was neglected, and it has become a plutocracy, less deferential but even less protected by democratic procedures.

There are many ways of being an active citizen, but for me being a Liberal Democrat is one way in which to address this central concern. I joined the Party as a foundation member in 1988. Given this background, I can perhaps explain the significance of membership of this party for me through the issue of constitutional reform, particularly proportional representation. 'First past the post' is not only unfair; it is irrational. It squanders knowledge and experience. Huge ranges of opinion are contorted to be crammed into just two main parties; these parties, sustained by alternating minorities of the electorate, enjoy and are corrupted by monopolies of power. 'The House of Commons', as Tony Wright, one of the newer Labour MPs observes, 'engages in about as much mutual learning as a football terrace'. As well as being equitable, PR facilitates mutual learning and combined policy development.

These processes are essential for dealing with all the major issues facing us, especially the well-being of life on the planet, and since they transcend national boundaries, the learning has also to be international (through the European Union and beyond). As yet Liberal Democrats accept these principles more readily than other parties. It is a party that believes, against the grain of a now dangerously brutish British tradition, that power must be shared. It is the only major party that does not assume that the only thing wrong is the others.

Brian Groombridge is Professor Emeritus of Adult Education, University of London; trustee, the Scarman Trust, Rights and Humanity (UK). Formerly IBA Head of Educational Programmes; Chairman, arts and broadcasting policy working group.

SPENCER HAGARD

The Liberals (and latterly the Liberal Democrats) have been the only party to have provided me with an environment which has felt like political home – a place with like spirits and shelter from a harsher world, generous in its view of human endeavour and frailty but tough and demanding to live in.

In my youth, I developed a political credo which has determined the political parties to which I might lend support and those which are anathema to me. My credo is the ideal of an equality of birthright, which I consider as an entitlement to everybody on earth of fundamental rights and requiring of them corresponding responsibilities, notably:

- to live in freedom under the law, to be able to associate freely with others, without fear of harassment, and regardless of racial origin, political or religious belief, or social class, and to afford the same to fellow citizens;
- to develop their individual potential to the fullest possible extent, through education and social opportunities, and in return to provide society with the benefits of their personal blossoming;
- to receive material sufficiency to meet not only their basic needs but to enable them to fulfil the responsibility of participating fully in society;

- to enjoy gainful and dignified employment, and to participate to the fullest possible extent in the ownership and management of the enterprise for which they worked;
- to participate fully in the management of society, through elected government operating at appropriate levels of social organisation from neighbourhood to global, through a fair and representative electoral system and through complete freedom of information.

The principles on which my youthful credo was based identified me with the then Liberal Party, in later years embracing newer liberal ideas (such as gay rights, and environmentalism), and providing the basis on which Liberals, and latterly Liberal Democrats, have for decades been active in many of the radical and progressive movements in British politics, such as:

- anti-racism (from the 1950s);
- gay rights and gender equality (from the 1960s);
- environmentalism (from the 1970s);
- opposition to tyranny in former Yugoslavia (from the 1980s);
- systematic constitutional reform (since forever);
- internationalism (since forever).

Though there have been many allies in many of these causes, almost none has been with us in all of them. That fact particularly distinguishes Liberal Democrats – as vehement in our opposition to Soviet tyranny as to apartheid, as determined upon establishing workers' rights in industrial ownership and management as to removing industrial relations from the grip of shop stewards – ever concerned to refer back to fundamental principles and to argue the trade-offs between them rather than accept the expedient. It looks to me like a good way for intelligent, sentient beasts to start facing the challenges of the next century too.

Spencer Hagard is a 53 year old public health consultant; he joined the Liberal Party while at medical school in St Andrews, was Chief Executive of the Health Education Authority from 1987 to 1994, and now advises a number of European governments, WHO and the World Bank on health and health services.

LADY HAMWEE

In what will be a selection of high-minded pieces, will this confession lower the tone too much? I joined the Liberal Party for largely social reasons.

I had campaigned (on the 'pro' side) in the European referendum in 1975, and after plucking up the courage to volunteer – I had never thought of myself as political – found that leafleting on street corners with like-minded people was fun. Soon after, I moved to Richmond upon Thames and sought out the liberals, hoping to get to meet people with whom I would have something in common.

I should have known that helping at jumble sales would be followed – seamlessly – by standing for the council. My parents – readers of the *Manchester Guardian* and the *News Chronicle,* to give an idea of my background – had described how my father returned from his first meeting of the Party, saying he couldn't go again; within 20 minutes they had asked him to chair the branch, within 40 were suggesting he stand for Manchester Council, and by the end were talking about Westminster.

I was lucky to find myself living in an area where the Liberals were developing so rapidly. And seeing at close quarters the complacency of a number of Tories, unable to understand that their old ways were not necessarily the only ways ('Why aren't you one of us?' I was asked soon after I was elected. 'After all, you wear a camel coat.'), while working with a number of energetic and idealistic colleagues, confirmed my undeveloped instinct that there was a lot to do to help make things better, and it need not be through paternalism or at the expense of individuality.

That hope of making friends has been met more than I could ever have expected: from fighting that first local election with a very few chums (so few we had to start delivering the good morning leaflet at 1am, and thought it good fun), to the close relationships, never to be broken, of those of us who struggled with our first budget after winning the council mid-term, to the camaraderie of the Lords. There I have the enormous privilege of listening to colleagues who can express the philosophy of our Party in a way I never could.

Sally Hamwee is a councillor on the London Borough of Richmond upon Thames; House of Lords spokesperson on environment: local government, housing and planning; President, Association of Liberal Democrat Councillors.

JOSEPHINE HAYES

Why am I involved in politics at all? Most people aren't. Until 1982 I wasn't either. Politics seemed stale and corrupt. As for parliament, it was an embarrassment. Were those people really in charge? Were those rituals serious? Why the battle rhetoric? And why so few women?

But I thought: politics are how people make things they want happen. If I want to put things right that need putting right, I had better get involved.

Why am I in the Liberal Democrats? There isn't a lot of competition!

Labour is at perpetual war between its extreme left and its moderates; the result is daft decisions. And its power structures deny individuals a voice. Labour missed two great chances to reform itself: in 1975, when Europe was tearing it apart, and in 1981, when many of its brightest and best left for the SDP.

I share the Conservatives' wish for stability and order, but not their defining characteristic: fear of change. I fear things staying the same!

A democracy needs thoughtful debate about all aspects of itself. In the Liberal Democrats, every member (man or woman) is heard and respected. Our ideas are the most creative and progressive. And people are learning to trust us. If our sympathisers in the other camps joined us, the transformation of politics would be swift and complete.

Josephine Hayes went from an ordinary background to read Greats at Oxford University, where she encountered the British class system in its full glory. She joined the SDP in 1982. She is currently Chair of Women Liberal Democrats and practises as a barrister in London.

LIZ HILL

Why am I a Liberal Democrat? The answer lies partly in the experience of not being one – namely the increasing impossibility from the mid 1970s onwards of voting *for* as opposed to *against* either of the large parties. In part it lies in the coincidence that the Liberal Democrats shared my views on the importance of certain issues. But there are also other reasons.

The Liberal Democrat analysis of the interlinking between our adversarial, unrepresentative and alienating political system and the

United Kingdom's persistent inability to reverse its sickening economic decline rang loud bells with me. This came after witnessing the spectacle from the vantage point of twelve years' work at the National Economic Development Office. I am still convinced that constitutional reform is a necessary, though not of course sufficient, condition for long-term reversal of decline. Willingness by native private sector companies to invest in this country as well as abroad depends upon it. Inward investment is not enough.

Measuring up to the seismic changes in the balance between capital and labour brought about by the microchip and information technology revolutions is a tall order for any political party, but it must be done if democracy and any decency of life for the majority is to survive. The Liberal Democrats stand a better chance of rising to the challenge than the other parties because we are unconstrained by excessive respect for the private sector, yet we do understand and respect it; nor are we hampered by contempt for the public sector or trade unions. We see that reformed trade unions and a properly deployed public sector have increased, not diminished, roles to play in the painful process of making major adjustments to the way in which we all earn our livings and pensions, as of course does access to appropriate education, training and retraining.

Also very important in making and keeping me a Liberal Democrat has been the deep thought, humanity and realism which have gone into the Liberal Democrats' appreciation of the fundamental values of liberty, equality and community.

We see the need to balance these against each other, to qualify each by reference to the others. Balance is vital to prevent liberty and individualism turning into licence. It is required to make sure that well-intentioned drives to reduce anti-social degrees of inequality do not tip over into unwarranted suppression of liberty. And to ensure that efforts to nourish the muscles of community do not create a mindless collectivism which stifles individual nonconformity. Respect for the individual is key. By encouraging individual self-worth, we encourage everyone to contribute by their own actions to improving society.

Such emphasis on the need to strike a balance between desirable social goals enables me to trust this group of human beings – as fallible as any other – not to fall into the trap of dogma and ideology, of which I have had a horror ever since studying the excesses of Calvin's Geneva and the religious wars of the 16th and 17th centuries. Ideas yes, ideology no!

Believing that this country badly needs greater fairness, as well as more freedom and openness, I like to think that I can help other Liberal Democrats in their task of building and safeguarding a fair, free and open society .... in which no-one shall be enslaved by poverty, ignorance or conformity.

Liz Hill was an industrial adviser at the National Economic Development Office until it was closed in 1992. Mainly a London local party worker, she was a member of the women policy working group 1993–1994.

LORD HOLME

I am a Liberal Democrat – just as I am a liberal – because I am an optimist; perhaps a cock-eyed optimist but nevertheless, despite all the horrid evidence to the contrary, persuaded of the hope of humanity.

This translates into a sense of wonder at the infinite possibilities of the journey which is undertaken by each individual being and by the human race itself. So I mistrust ideologists who want to prescribe the destination, trying to cramp all that might happen into the small coffin of what they think should happen. Far better to set out as if for an adventure, armed only with the compass of liberal human values and the map of inherited wisdom.

That last point means books, of course. Ah, the books! Do we choose them or do they choose us? Suffice it to say if I ever thought I could escape from liberalism, the books stand around me in a tall circle telling me to stay.

From the pages of Bunyan to Blake, from Milton and Mill, Paine and Popper, and from many, many others, the sprite of freedom dances before my eyes. But always a freedom balanced by responsibility for others, by social feeling and communal well-being, and not the freedom of callous selfishness or indifference, of which we see so much evidence around us.

The quest for such freedom is an endless journey, and liberals are lucky to have each others' company on the way.

Richard Holme was Director of the Campaign for Electoral Reform 1976–85; President of the Liberal Party 1980–81; candidate for Cheltenham 1983 and 1987;

election manifesto coordinator 1992. Made a life peer in 1990, he is currently spokesman on Northern Ireland, and general election campaign director.

CLLR DAVID HOWARTH

No-one shall be enslaved by poverty, ignorance or conformity

A phrase from the preamble of the old Liberal Party's constitution, now happily transferred to the Liberal Democrats', says best what Liberal Democrats stand for. Liberals, it declares, work to build a society in which 'no-one shall be enslaved by poverty, ignorance or conformity.'

Not even the opening page of Mill's *On Liberty,* with its assertion that no-one should be coerced except to prevent harm to others, expresses so accurately the essence of Liberal politics. Liberalism is not just a shield to ward off an over-mighty state. It is a sword, a weapon for change towards a distinctive, and distinctively better, society.

Poverty

Plainly, economic improvement is not a distinctively liberal aim. But ensuring that none shall be *enslaved* by poverty is. It focuses not on increasing material wealth for its own sake, but on eliminating the repression poverty causes. Poverty prevents people from being free – free to make choices and even, when the struggle just to survive is paramount, to think their own thoughts.

This focus on the political effects of poverty, rather than just on inequality, allows Liberal Democrats to hold wide, non-materialistic views of economic questions. It allows, for example, advanced views on environmental protection. Conventional measures of prosperity notwithstanding, where the environment has been destroyed, vast numbers of people experience conditions politically equivalent to absolute poverty. Where the struggle to ward off ill-health and to find physical safety become all-important, freedom, autonomy and dignity disappear. But the same non-materialistic view inoculates Liberal Democrats against claims that any sacrifice of liberty is worthwhile if it increases material well-being. Material welfare, including health, is a means to an end, not the end itself.

Ignorance

Creating a society free of ignorance dominates Liberal Democrat thinking to an extraordinary degree, from the Party's central 1990s sound-bite – 'a penny on income tax for education' – to opposition to censorship and support for open government and freedom of information.

Liberals still believe in what is fashionably called the 'Enlightenment project'. Not only should everyone be capable of participating in political discussion, but also reason and knowledge, especially scientific knowledge, should form the basis of that discussion. Liberals instinctively reject the reliance on traditional authority and the cynical manipulation of myth and superstition fundamental to conservatism, including its modern 'communitarian' forms.

Critics say that the Enlightenment project has led to arrogant and ultimately disastrous attempts, such as Marxism, to claim to apply scientific methods to politics. But Liberals have never claimed, as socialists did, that they possess knowledge that authorises them to reconstruct society. They claim instead only that a society is rational to the extent that its members debate its future in a rational way.

Critics also say that the Enlightenment project leads all values to dissolve into relativism. But there is a big difference between saying that there is no moral and political truth, as relativists claim, and saying that although objective truth exists, we cannot be certain what it is, and so the state should not impose all-embracing moral, religious or political views. Indeed, relativism underpins not liberalism but its enemies, the power-worshipping doctrines of Leninism and fascism and the reactionary inertia of 'post-modernism'.

Conformity

Creating a society where no-one is enslaved by conformity is perhaps the most distinctive liberal aim of all. It expresses a fundamental commitment to protecting individuality. Human creativity is the ultimate resource, and its shackling by convention and prejudice the ultimate extravagance. Moreover, this same aim is central to the Liberal Democrat conception of human rights. Freedom of speech and religion are forms of the freedom to be different.

But freedom from ignorance and freedom from conformity counterbalance each other. Traditional authority is subject to rational criticism, not to romantic but irrational revolt. Freedom from enslavement by conformity means not that it is wrong to criticise others, only that it is wrong to criticise others because they are acting unconventionally. Ignorance of the consequences of one's actions for others is one of the most serious forms of ignorance. Liberalism is for individuality, not individualism – at least if individualism means that existential individualism in which no-one is accountable to anyone else.

Ultimately, one can divide political ideologies into those that appeal to fantasies of control and those that appeal to fantasies of liberation. Socialism appeals to people offended by the disorganisation of markets and by apparently never-ending political debate. Liberalism, in contrast, appeals to those who wish themselves and others to be free.

David Howarth, who leads the Liberal Democrat group on Cambridge City Council, has represented local councillors on the party's Federal Policy Committee since 1989. He teaches law at the University of Cambridge and has been a Fellow of Clare College, Cambridge since 1985.

SIMON HUGHES MP

I am a Liberal Democrat because the Liberal Democrats are the best political home for liberals in the UK in the 1990s.

I believe in the preamble to our party constitution – which, put simply for me, means internationalism, environmentalism, civil liberties, the maximum dispersal of power and a pragmatic view about the best way of running our economy.

I believe in the triple political aspiration of liberty, equality and community. I am a pluralist. No one party or person has the monopoly of political truth or wisdom - and developing political systems which enable all individuals and groups to be as influential as possible is a centally important political conviction.

But as well as being a Liberal Democrat by conviction I am a Liberal Democrat from experience.

I am in favour of the greatest dispersal of wealth and power. That is why I oppose the Conservative Party – because in practice they are dogmatic about the merits of the private over the public, and because in practice they regularly preside over the continuingly unequal distributions in our society, to the unjustified disadvantage of many of our fellow citizens.

I am also in favour of the maximum diversity of economic, social and political relationships. This is why I do not support the Labour Party (old or new) – because in practice so many of them are still not pluralists, and still have a dogmatic view about the rightness of only one political way forward, and because in practice they so often manifest partisanship, not independence, and self-interested pragmatism, not principles.

Liberal Democracy is a political philosophy gaining in support and importance the world over. It is a set of interlinked values and principles which have stood the test of time and experience and have been vindicated by the benefits they have produced.

This liberal will be a Liberal Democrat for as long as the party of the same name preaches – and more importantly practices – liberal democracy to empower people. The test of our success is how well we overcome the poverty, ignorance and conformity which it is the duty of radical politicians to challenge.

Simon Hughes has been the MP for Southwark & Bermondsey since 1983. He was environment spokesman from 1988–95, and is now health spokesman.

CHRISTOPHER HUHNE

Although I came to the Liberal Democrats through the SDP, I am increasingly drawn to the liberal strand of the party's philosophical roots. Liberalism puts people and their freedoms first. I am a liberal because I believe that people should be free from the undue influence of any concentration of power, whether it is big government, big business or big trade unions. Indeed, liberal societies are often those where power is so diffused and counter-balanced that few people really wield it at all, except in circumstances of dire national emergency. That seems to me to be an ideal to strive for: a society in which no-one is afraid of their boss, because they can easily find work elsewhere; where no-one is afraid of the police because of the excellence of the complaints procedure; where no-one is afraid of a press baron, because there are many other television stations and newspapers not under his sway.

Another reason for being a liberal is the belief in reason and toleration. The civilised society should not be judged solely by the conditions of life for its conventional and ordinary members, but by the tolerance it extends to its minorities, rebels and misfits. Clearly, people cannot enjoy freedoms at the expense of others' freedoms, so there is always a balance. But there ought to be the widest possible freedom for individuals consistent with protecting the freedoms of others. Liberal societies are diverse, open, pluralistic. And fun.

That stress on freedoms to do things does not mean that I am a Gladstonian believer in the night-watchman state. The state is the organised expression of society, and its role is crucial in a liberal society. If the individual is at the centre of our concerns, it is essential that people should have equal opportunities because otherwise they cannot develop their individuality. At the same time, everyone should enjoy freedom from want. A rich society that cannot provide shelter, clothing and food for all its members is failing. Without that commitment to freedom from want, other freedoms become meaningless. The state thus has an enabling role, but liberals must always beware the ability of any government to define its own narrow interests – as a bureaucracy or a political class – as those of society as a whole. Governments and bureaucracies can be as self-serving as any other interest group.

Christopher Huhne is an economist assessing countries borrowing on the international capital markets after a long career as an economic columnist for the Guardian *and the* Independent on Sunday. *He chaired the Party's press and broadcasting policy working group and fought Reading East in 1983 and Oxford West & Abingdon in 1987.*

SIR ANTHONY JACOBS

I first became a Liberal Party activist in 1972, which enabled me to fight as parliamentary candidate for Watford in the two 1974 general elections. I hoped and believed that under the leadership of Jeremy Thorpe this would be the first Liberal breakthrough since the war. I believed that as an experienced businessman I might have something to offer on improving the social security and tax system and encouragement of small businesses.

At that time there was a desperate housing shortage, even worse than today, and I believed that more radical ideas were needed to improve the situation of the homeless and of those young married couples forced to live with their families. It was not difficult to support the Liberal Party when I so strongly believed in the rights of the individual and always distrusted the use of power by large businesses and large trade unions. I particularly distrusted the dogmatic opinions of the extremist elements of the other parties; nothing has changed.

I was aware of the unjustness of the electoral system and hoped that in due course it would be changed. However, after four more general elections had passed I came to realise that even if our vote significantly increased, as it did in 1983 when we almost equalled Labour's vote, our parliamentary position would barely advance at all. I have always strongly supported proportional representation and today I believe that this is the single most important objective for the Liberal Democrats.

Many arguments are given in favour of electoral reform, but to me one argument supersedes all others; that in the 1992 general election, for every million people who voted Tory, they were rewarded with 24 members of parliament; for every million people who voted Labour, they were rewarded with 23 members of parliament; for every million people who voted Liberal Democrat, they were rewarded with 3 members of parliament. This is an injustice of mega proportions. Why should the votes of a Liberal Democrat voter be worth only a fraction of those of a Tory or Labour voter? Under the present system six million liberals have been effectively disenfranchised.

Today I try to ensure that all my work within the Party will advance to some degree the opportunity for us to change the electoral system. Without that change we shall remain for ever powerless within parliament.

Sir Anthony Jacobs is aged 64 and married with two children; he is a chartered accountant; former owner of the British School of Motoring; Joint Treasurer of the Liberal Party 1984–87; Vice President Social & Liberal Democrats 1988.

GEORGINA JAMES

Liberal Democracy is not a political ideology. It is rather a cast of mind which balances high ideals with common sense; which is committed to a system of moral values and yet strives for tolerance and pluralism within it; which believes in the rule of law, but is repelled by authoritarianism. In fact, you do not join the Liberal Democrats. You just discover that you are one.

Political groups have traditionally been centred on vested interests but the core of Liberal Democracy is conscience. Or rather thousands of individual consciences reaching a conclusion on best action after thorough debate.

This consensus approach does not fit with either our unfair voting system, nor with the fake polarisation of the House of Commons where still, small voices of calm are rarely heard.

We know, therefore, that it will not be easy to create Vaclav Havel's vision of 'a new type of human community' which will transcend primitive tribal and nationalistic instincts. We also realise it will take time for people to recognise the weakness of didacticism and the strength of intelligent compromise.

But down the centuries the golden threads of reason and altruism weave unbroken through the history of mankind's actions and aspirations. We are comforted. We are hopeful. We can wait.

Georgina James is a businesswoman, and was Euro-candidate for Essex West & Hertfordshire East in 1994.

SIR RUSSELL JOHNSTON MP

I came to liberalism as a student, joining the Party in 1954. British liberalism was almost at its nadir. In Scotland, in 1955, we could only field five candidates for 71 seats! It was beyond my imagination that I should be an MP ten years later. Ambition was not a motivation!

My reasons were both intellectual and emotional: it seemed to me then, and still does, that liberalism was the only political philosophy which fitted together, seamlessly, these two driving elements of the human personality. Fitted them together and provided a frame within which society could evolve harmoniously and productively.

It concentrated on the primacy of the individual. It made the assumption that if we concentrated on him or her, justice for the group of which he or she is a part would follow logically, while the converse was untrue. This fundamentally set it apart from political philosophies, like communism, socialism and nationalism, which started from the opposite pole, sought to better the group, and believed that this would lead, in time, to the improvement of the individual's lot. Conservatism is not really a philosophy, but a resistance to change, valuable in clarifying arguments about the way we are to go, but valueless in providing signposts. Often it is little more than a consensus of prejudices moderated by remorse.

At the beginning, I was much influenced by John Stuart Mill – whose reasoned arguments are still a delight to read – and the Yorkshire Liberal, Elliot Dodds, who defined liberalism as 'Liberty, welfare and responsibility'. But, in Scotland, I was hugely inspired by John Bannerman, the Scottish Liberal Leader, who was a man of irrepressible, untidy kindness. He taught me that politics was not only about devising rules, but enabling exceptions. And that the openness and cooperation, which an individual-based philosophy required, could only work with compassion.

He also introduced me to federalism, as the only means of resolving the conflicting demands for regional and national identity on the one hand and wider political, economic and social integration on the other. They were arguments as applicable to the United Kingdom as to the European Community and across the Atlantic in Canada, as I found from the writings of Canadian Liberal Leader, Pierre Elliot Trudeau.

The international nature of liberalism was quickly borne in upon me and it was exciting to realise how universal were the tenets of the liberal faith. Because of PR, most continental liberal parties were at some time or other in coalition government. The great, warm, patient Giovanni Malagodi taught me that compromise was no betrayal of principle – the traditional British confrontational position with which even liberals were often infected – but a step or two on the march towards one's goals.

Being brought up in the Highlands of Scotland, long neglected by successive governments, I was an instinctive Keynesian, and the proposition for a Highlands & Islands Development Board was based on the 1928 Liberal

Yellow Book. The fact that one opposed excessive state control – of which the logical outcome for most of my life was the Soviet Union – did not mean that one was afraid of the state; one recognised it had benign and necessary functions, of which development was one, the protection of the weak another, the provision of certain universal public services another. John Kenneth Galbraith summed it all up in his magnificent speech on liberalism to the Liberal International Congress in Ottawa in 1987.

There are certain words that have a liberal resonance, not exclusively, but predominantly .... fairness, openness, tolerance, compassion; I do not find them so well represented in other political philosophies.

Sir Russell Johnston has been MP for Inverness (now Inverness, Nairn & Lochaber) since 1964. He was Deputy Leader of the Liberal Democrats, 1988-92, and is currently spokesman on eastern and central Europe, and Leader of the Liberal, Democrat and Reform group in the Council of Europe.

CLLR TREVOR JONES

Liberalism is founded on two admirable viewpoints. One emphasises the value of other people and glories in the great variety of their different contributions to our life together. The other doesn't take oneself too seriously!

Furthermore, while it has always advanced the need for each of us to strive to make the most of our life, it wants our enterprise to be for the common good, not just our own.

Trevor Jones is the Managing Director of Liberal Democrat Publications and a former Mayor of Casterbridge.

CLLR RICHARD KEMP

It may sound trite, or even totally concocted, but one of the first memories I have is thinking that it was a great shame that the Seventh Cavalry always beat the Indians in the 1950s movies which were always on the television when I was five or six years old. I just did not think that it was fair.

Fairness is not a word that is used much in politics these days. Perhaps it is too subjective or perhaps just too wishy-washy. But it is, nevertheless, at the heart of my political philosophy. I don't think it fair that some people get £1,000,000 a year to live on whilst others live on the breadline. I don't think it fair that some people live in cardboard city whilst others live in opulence just around the corner. I don't think it fair that some people are born to poverty, either in this country or in most of the countries of the world, while others are born to consume ten times as much of the world's resources.

Having decided that I wanted to fight unfairness I found the sight of most political parties unedifying. I have never believed that Labour have wanted to share things more fairly. The Labour Party has always been a right wing party dedicated to redistributing the spoils to a different elite. Communism was always doomed to failure.

But I did not choose liberalism for negative reasons. I could have done like others and decided to work for a pressure group or become a 'social worker'. What attracted me to the liberal fight against unfairness was the belief that it could and should be done from the bottom up. Liberalism inherently believes that almost everyone has the capacity to run their own lives and should be given the freedom to do it. It also believes that, given the freedom, most people will act responsibly and not become greedy and try to take out more than their due.

The more I do, the more I believe this. I represent an inner city ward and work in deprived areas. The amazing thing about these areas is the resilience of the people who live in them. Circumstances that would defeat most people are stoically endured and overcome by these residents. Give them some power to change their lives and they do not abuse it but use it sensitively for the general good.

From housing cooperatives to workers cooperatives, from real neighbourhood councils to agricultural communes, 'bottom up' has been seen to work. 'Bottom up' really challenges the system. It allows people to be individual, to sort out their futures, to lead their own lifestyles.

Can you imagine what our country would feel like if was not run by benevolent (or otherwise) despots in Whitehall, but was a democracy led by people on more than a 'once in four years basis'? It would be very, very different from the country we live in. It would not be polluted and grey and full of tower blocks and featureless shopping centres and dangerous to walk in. It would be green, concerned and caring.

Others share some of our beliefs. They believe in internationalism, although not quite in the same way as we do. They believe in the environment. They even believe in regional government. But we are unique in devising a political system which links the concept of fairness to an ideology which says not that: 'Jack is as good as his master' but rather: 'Jack should be his own master'.

Richard Kemp is a Liverpool City Councillor, PPC for Wavertree and a member of the Federal Policy Committee.

SIR LUDOVIC KENNEDY

Had the postwar Liberal Party leader, Clement Davies, been a more charismatic character, I might have joined the Liberal Party earlier; but it wasn't until Jo Grimond succeeded Davies as the Party's leader in 1956 that I instinctively knew that his was a mast I could nail my colours to. What his thoughts on detailed policies were I did not know, but what captivated me were his happy demeanour, trenchant wit and aura of natural leadership; and although an ITN newscaster at the time, and therefore outwardly nonpolitical, I wrote to congratulate him and offer my support.

When the ludicrous Anthony Eden mistook Nasser for Hitler by colluding secretly with Israel to invade Egypt, I felt an imperative urge to enter the fray, and when the Rochdale byelection came up a little later, I volunteered to stand and was accepted. In the event I lost the byelection by 4,500 votes and in the general election the following year by 2,700. But on both occasions Jo Grimond, Jeremy Thorpe and other of the six Liberal MPs came up to speak for me, and I knew I had found my true political home.

What is it that makes us all liberals or social democrats? A free market economy, a compassionate attitude to social problems and a readiness always to see the need for radical reform; and underpinning all this an inclination to take the side of the individual against the big battalions. In my own case that has resulted in speaking up for those too inarticulate or too crushed to speak for themselves, at least with any conviction; victims of miscarriages of criminal justice and those in torment from terminal illness who long to die but whose doctors are prevented by the law (and by most Tory MPs) from helping them to do so officially (though more and more are prepared to risk the consequences by doing so unofficially). On this last head I submitted a motion to the 1995 Liberal Democrat conference calling for a Royal Commission on voluntary euthanasia. The Conference Committee threw it out. But I hope they will not continue to do so. It will come in time, and is a liberal reform if any is.

Ludovic Kennedy's books have helped to right several miscarriages of justice. He is the President of the Voluntary Euthanasia Society.

CLLR EVELYN KNOWLES

Well, I could not be anything else. I came late to politics, angry at what I saw about me but not knowing how to change things. I became caught up in the euphoria of the SDP, new beginnings and all that – and my toe was in the water of politics.

As I took part in the SDP's rise and fall, its decanting, its exfoliation, I met Liberals of long standing. I began to learn the feelings and the messages behind the policies, and I found my place.

I could never be a Tory; their lack of principles and the examples they have set in all their years of government are, to me, unacceptable.

I could never join Labour. Growing up, as I did, in Bow and Bethnal Green in the '30s and '40s, I often wondered why there were never any improvements in our environment. I now know.

I am proud to be a Liberal Democrat who has the opportunity to contribute to my Party's policies; who has a say in how it is run; who can feel confident that the policies we believe in are for the benefit of all; who knows that I am supported in working with local people and getting their voices heard.

That's why.

Evelyn Knowles is a Liberal Democrat activist, feminist and cycling woman.

BILL LE BRETON

A very liberal haiku

Because restrictions rankle
boundaries limit
privilege petrifies
poverty paralyses
borders divide
discrimination deadens
fear frustrates
ignorance imprisons
conformity constrains
class encrusts
myth enshrouds
duty deforms
authority anaesthetises
Let me love liberty
trust tolerance
explore experience
encourage equality
enjoy justice
challenge convention
crave community
give generously
value individuality
spread concern
relish reason
pursue peace
demand democracy

Bill le Breton is Chair of the Association of Liberal Democrat Councillors. Japanese verse is only a passing interest; in the real world, he is married with two young children, plays cricket on Wednesday evenings for Rimington village cricket club and, all too infrequently, is 'second' on a climbing rope behind Tony Greaves. His biography is longer than his contribution - a politican of his age.

DEEPA KOREA

Liberal Democracy balances freedom and individual choice with the need for civic responsibility.

It offers me effectiveness in place of indifference.

It gives me a real alternative to false assurances.

And it provides me with the opportunity for change.

I relish the challenge of contributing to such a dynamic and radical force for change through my support of the Liberal Democrats.

Deepa Korea is Assistant Community Relations Adviser, Royal Borough of Kensington and Chelsea; she was formerly the ethnic minorities researcher to Paddy Ashdown MP.

LORD LESTER

I am a lifelong liberal because I cherish individualism and self-government, and seek to resist the conforming pressures of a mass society. My values have been influenced by the lessons of the Holocaust and of colonial oppression, and my work in combating race and sex discrimination and promoting press freedom.

I became a Liberal Democrat because my idea of democracy depends upon nourishing a culture of liberty as well as promoting equality. I distrust concentrations of power, whether in the hands of the state and its agents or in the hands of 'private governments'. I believe in the need for effective safeguards against the misuse of power, for effective remedies where basic human rights and freedoms are violated, and for freedom of public information about the way in which power is exercised in our name.

I agree with the late Professor HLA Hart's definition of the fallacy of moral populism, namely, 'that the majority have a moral right to dictate how all should live. This is a misunderstanding of democracy which still menaces individual liberty .... The central mistake is a failure to distinguish the acceptable principle that political power is best entrusted to the majority from the unacceptable claim that what the majority do with that power is beyond criticism and must never be resisted.'

Like my fellow Liberal Democrats, what I seek, in terms of the reform of our outmoded and ethically aimless constitutional arrangements, is government which is both democratic and limited by law. In my view, government should be limited by the supreme law of a modern and coherent British constitution, protecting civil and political rights, allocating powers to democratically elected national and regional legislative authorities, and local authorities, to which executive governing bodies are genuinely accountable.

Such a constitution would be based upon popular sovereignty and the premise that power should be exercised at the lowest level compatible with good government. It would reflect and promote universal values enshrined in the European Union and in international human rights codes. It would reform both Houses of Parliament. It would ensure that the outcome of elections fairly reflects the people's choices. It would guarantee judicial independence. And it would abolish arbitrary prerogative powers.

We Liberal Democrats are unique as a British political party in standing for these principles and in striving to attain them.

Anthony Lester QC is a practising barrister and a working Liberal Democrat peer, campaigning for constitutional and law reform.

CLIVE LINDLEY

I came to the Liberal Democrats via the Labour Party and the SDP – and have no regrets!

Raised in a Tory family, it took the experience of two years military service for me to become politically aware and appalled at Tory attitudes. That brought me into the Labour Party as an activist in my early 20s, becoming in due course a constituency chairman and a parliamentary candidate.

In parallel with political activism, I was also busy founding a business of a national and international character. The companies I ran had more than 1,000 employees, and I always accepted the justice and good sense of workers' representation through trade unions. As a result of annual negotiations, and my attendance at Labour's annual party conferences, I got to know the most senior leaders of the two large unions that organised within my group of companies.

It was in the late 1970s, over a glass of champagne in the convivial Yate's Wine Lodge in Blackpool, that a senior union leader informed me with no possibility of contradiction that: 'the Labour Party had no serious function other than to be the political arm of the trade unions'. That was just before the winter of discontent!

Combining this revelation with their myopic anti-Europeanism and absurd unilateralism brought me to the end of the road with Labour. I could no longer continue to work or vote for a party that represented such a dangerously lunatic position.

I was enthusiastic for the SDP and for the Alliance. Indeed, I was early an active proponent of the merger with the Liberals. It seemed to me after 1983 that since both parties had fought together in the general election on the same manifesto, not only was it tactically sensible that this new political force should be seen to be united, but that it would be intellectually dishonest to pretend that the two parties any longer represented separate things – except perhaps the alternative of two leaders, and we saw the trouble that that got us into in 1987!

I was a strong supporter of the merger and am happy to belong to a non-class based party which represents a maturity of judgement in its policies, together with balance and fairness. For the future, I fear for our country with its insular attitudes and the hegemony of an appalling tabloid press which now sets the political agenda.

There are so many dangers in our steadily failing system, principally the lack of realisation that unless we keep wealth creation at the forefront of our concerns, we will never have the means to pay for the kind of progressive society that we so earnestly desire.

Fundamentally, though, until we have fair voting and can reform the elective dictatorship of governments representing only the largest minority at any election, then we will fail to get to grips with the many and varied reforms that our social and political system is crying out for. Only the Liberal Democrats so far appear to have understood that.

Clive Lindley is a businessman and was formerly Chairman SDP Trustees; Alliance parliamentary (twice), Euro-parliamentary (once), candidate; Chair of Finance, Liberal Democrats; member, Federal Executive.

GORDON LISHMAN

I am a Liberal Democrat because I am a liberal; the Liberal Democrats are my political home.

I am a liberal because I believe that generosity of spirit and commitment to personal freedom should be the guiding principles of political philosophy.

I am fortunate in my certainty and in the comfort I find in the humanist liberal tradition. In 1965, Jo Grimond advised me – and a whole conference of Young Liberals – to read the essay *On Liberty* once a year. I am still delighted by the extent to which I feel wholly at home in the centre of that tradition.

Its key elements are the commitment to personal liberation and fulfilment, combined with active tolerance, founded in the will and ability to identify with others. These principles lead to the liberal principles of the rule of law and the belief in the active use of liberty, involving ourselves and others in taking, using and sharing power and responsibility for our own lives. They involve the intelligent and compassionate use of the state's machinery to support those who need assistance and to guarantee fairness. These principles are the opposite and enemy of conservatism.

Liberalism is a *philosophy:* a set of mutually reinforcing beliefs brought coherently together in a view of life and personal conduct. To be effective, liberalism also needs to be an *ideology:* that is, to add three further elements:

1. understanding and *analysis* of its current context, the world it inhabits;
2. a *programme* to change society (not just a plan for parliamentary legislation); and
3. the *strategy* for achieving that change (not just for winning office).

I shall be a happier Liberal Democrat when my Party fully and publicly acknowledges the liberalism that is its philosophical core and accepts the need for a thorough, clear and radical ideology.

Gordon Lishman has been an active liberal since 1963. He is the Operations Director of Age Concern and occupies his political time in working with the Federal Liberal Democrats.

CLLR CLIVE LLOYD

Having voted Liberal for many years, mainly as an anti-Tory vote, I thought that I should at least read about the policies of the Liberal Party to discover what I was actually voting for. Upon reading the policy documents I was pleased to find that my views were, in the main, the policies of the Liberal Party:

The Liberal Party's belief that both sides of industry, management and employee, could improve production, profits and a better living standard for all by meeting together and discussing matters that were important to the shop floor and to management; becoming aware of each other's problems and engendering a feeling of trust rather than the 'them and us' mistrust.

The Party's views on involving communities in the decision-making process felt far more democratic, as did the policy on proportional representation.

Encouraging expectations of the differing nationalities within the United Kingdom, so that Wales, Scotland and Northern Ireland could manage their own internal matters whilst having a voice in parliament and remaining within the United Kingdom, to me was sensible, and allowed the voice of minorities to be heard in a peaceful and democratic way.

The Liberal Democrats are to me, the one party that recognises the abilities of each individual to work for the betterment of themselves and the family unit, while assisting in the rebuilding of the nation through their own efforts, with the guidance and assistance of central government.

Clive Lloyd is a sacked GCHQ trade unionist and has been a councillor for eight years. He is chairman of an economic development regeneration committee, developing and regenerating deprived areas.

CLLR SARAH LUDFORD

Two phrases best sum up my political allegiance: 'Peace, Reform and Liberation' from our conference song *The Liberal March,* and our constitutional preamble 'No-one shall be enslaved by poverty, ignorance or conformity.'

I am a restless, sometimes angry, reformer who hates injustice and inefficiency equally. I am by nature a rebel and I dislike hierarchy, authoritarianism and patronage. When push comes to shove, I am on the side of the little people who get a raw deal in life.

I am stopped from being an anarchist by the knowledge that an absence of rules favours the strong, who will exploit the weak. But I dislike bureaucracy and unnecessary regulation, and insist that reason, not prejudice, habit, arbitrary power or vested interest should determine the rules. I want a level playing field, and am an economic liberal, preferring competition to regulation where possible.

Coupled with this reforming and liberationist conviction is, perhaps paradoxically, a strong dose of faith and hope in the prospect of a better way. I am a believer in people power, and fundamentally an optimist about the potential of people, either individually or together, to seek out improvements and find solutions to problems. From this comes my commitment to education and 'self-improvement'.

Although not religious, I believe there is a spiritual element in life, and I find inspiration in the force and strength of the human spirit. I find socialism and communism too bleak because of their denial of the optimistic, the humanistic and the spiritual in their deterministic materialism.

But I am wary of moralists, and I instinctively reject the fashionable 'communitarianism' because of its illiberal and anti-individualist undercurrents; it smacks of a patronising attempt to control the unruly masses. It also seems at root distrustful of people whereas I am fundamentally trustful and hopeful, celebrating people's energy, diversity and variety, and believing that most people will live up to the trust and expectation placed in them.

I am not a philosopher and I have never intellectualised my attachment to Liberal Democracy. My commitment is rooted in a combination of instinct and practical experience. I think if I was more of a theorist, and less suspicious of ideology, I might have joined the Labour Party, but my instinct and powers of observation about the patronising and hypocritical weaknesses of Labour warned me off. Theirs is not the route to empowerment and liberation.

The biggest and most important challenge for Liberal Democrats is to stop concentrations and abuses of power. We are the only major party for whom this is a prime determinant of policy, the others being driven mainly by economic analysis. That is why we do not fit the classic left–right linear spread, and prefer our own conservative–radical spectrum, on which Tories and Labour are closer to each other than either is to us.

I am a strong champion of social justice, compassion, and the validity of non-profit activities but also of economic enterprise, and of self help and hard work where possible. I do not find 'efficiency' and 'effectiveness' dirty capitalist words. I dislike Labour's tolerance, even encouragement, of sloppiness and low standards in the public sector (because of the priority it has always given to the producer interests) as much as I dislike Tory denigration of public sector values.

I value highly the civic sphere and people forming social and community networks which reflect and support a culture of robust citizenship. I strongly regret that, because the British are constitutionally subjects, this has a psychological as well as political effect in discouraging active and assertive citizenship, the protection of civil liberties, and government reform.

I have read a quotation from Chinese dissident Wei Jing-sheng with which I wholeheartedly agree: 'We want no more gods and emperors, no more saviours of any kind. Democracy, freedom and happiness are the only goals of modernisation.'

On the same day, I read of the Labour supporters whom Tony Blair is likely to wheel in to fill the top advisory and quango posts, and my radicalism – why I am a Liberal Democrat – is once again reinforced. Ours is an agenda which, unlike the others', which promise to run the existing system more benevolently, insists that only real change to the system can free the energies and talents of people from the bottom up.

Sarah Ludford joined the Liberal Party in 1981 in Brussels. She is a European and public affairs consultant, Islington councillor and Vice Chair of the Federal Policy Committee.

LIZ LYNNE MP

I am a Liberal Democrat because I believe, above all, in the freedom of the individual. I went to my first Young Liberal meeting when I was eleven, and they were talking about just that. I realise now that it was probably a discussion about the preamble to the Liberal Party constitution. I knew there and then that the Liberals were the party I wanted to support.

I had a very chequered childhood and was aware of people classed as 'outsiders' at a very early age, and I was determined that had to change. My mother brought my brother and I up with very little money but with a very strong sense of justice.

Part of my childhood was spent in a disabled person's home, as my mother was running it. Most of my friends at that time were disabled and I knew the discrimination they suffered and I was determined that I would fight for their rights and the rights of all of us who weren't part of the established 'norm'.

I felt comfortable being a Liberal then as I believe that it was the only party that really cared for the individual. I still believe that is the case today.

Liz Lynne has been MP for Rochdale since 1992 and is social security and disability spokesperson.

TERRY MAHER

In 1956, Britain's Conservative Government, under the leadership of Anthony Eden, became involved in the ill-fated 'Suez Crisis'. The Egyptian leader Colonel Nasser had nationalised the Suez Canal in July 1956, and Anglo-French forces invaded Egypt in October on the pretext of separating Egyptian and Israeli troops who were already in conflict. It was clear, however, that there had been collusion between the British, French and Israelis, and that the real purpose of the invasion was to retake the Canal. There was world-wide condemnation, not least from the United Nations and the United States. The whole enterprise was a fiasco, ended in ignominious withdrawal, and was deeply damaging to British interests.

Political passions in this country, however, were raised in a manner rarely seen before or since. Members of families were turned against each other. In some quarters it was thought treasonable to question any aspect of the 'adventure'. The Labour Party supported the Government in the early stages but later relented. The Liberal Party stood out in unequivocal condemnation.

For me the Suez crisis was a catalyst – I had to be involved in politics to seek to influence events, however remotely; and I was in no doubt that it was the Liberal Party in which I belonged. Jo Grimond had recently become leader and was articulating Liberal philosophy in a refreshingly relevant style. I wrote to the Manchester Liberal headquarters and asked to join the Party. It is a decision that I have never regretted, and in 1964 and 1966 I fought two general elections as a Liberal candidate.

Today, however, I would like to see the Liberal Democrats being bolder and more radical in their policies. We run the risk of trying too hard to look like a government (or opposition) in waiting.

I am increasingly concerned at the undemocratic centralisation and concentration of power in Whitehall, and at the lack of political will to reduce substantially, below 43 per cent, the proportion of what we earn which is spent by government.

Tinkering is not enough. We need to break down power and return it to democratically elected bodies; we need to question whether the state can any longer be a universal provider; and we need to change and simplify our tax system so, for example, it no longer distorts investment decisions which have far-reaching and damaging but publicly unrecognised consequences.

These issues will not be addressed by the Conservative or Labour Parties; they remain a challenge for the Liberal Democrats.

Terry Maher is a publisher, bookseller, and author. He developed Dillons into Britain's largest specialist bookseller, and he led the ultimately successful campaign to abolish price control on books.

PAUL MARSHALL

The central appeal of the Liberal Democrats, and before them of the SDP and of the Liberal Party, has always been that they have sought to reconcile the requirements of a free and open market economy with the principles of social justice. For the last 80 years this dual commitment has confined us to the sidelines of British politics whilst the two larger parties have slugged it out in the interests of either labour or capital.

But history is moving in our direction. The changes that have taken place over the past ten years, the debunking of socialism and the much more widespread acceptance of the market economy, the end of many of the rigidities in British society, and the much greater integration of Britain into the international economy are bringing to an end the artificial duality which has plagued British politics this century.

As society becomes more plural, so too will politics. This presents Liberal Democrats with our great opportunity. While the central Liberal Democrat quest to reconcile the free market with social justice has now become quasi-orthodoxy across the political spectrum, the issues which flow from that – investment in education to enable everyone to participate in the market economy, constitutional reform to make politics more reflective of an open and plural society, and welfare reform to ensure that we provide adequately for the victims of economic change – are rising to the top of the national agenda; and these issues are natural Liberal Democrat issues. Hopefully the 21st century will be our century.

Paul Marshall is Director of Mercury Asset Management PLC, responsible for European equity investments. He was research assistant to Charles Kennedy MP, 1984; parliamentary candidate, Fulham, 1987; Chairman, City Liberal Democrats since 1994.

CLLR CHRISTOPHER MASON

Habit.

I was converted in 1961 (at the age of 20) to supporting the Liberal Party by Jo Grimond's approach to the issues of the day, particularly the role of the United Nations in the Congo. I was interested in politics, idealistic about peace and justice, and instinctively against authority.

Thirty-five years on I keep going as a Liberal Democrat because I still believe in the values of liberalism and I can live with Liberal Democrat policies. After fourteen years as a regional councillor I have got used to politics as a way of life. I believe the Scottish Liberal Democrats will have a useful role to play in the Scottish Parliament which, because it will be elected by proportional representation, will give a real opportunity for Liberal Democrat values and ideas to be carried into action.

The essential point of political liberalism, for me, is to use the power of government to create a balance in society which gives as much opportunity as possible to both the needs of individuals and the needs of society as a whole. It is this balanced position which makes political liberalism the best starting point for dealing with environmental as well as social and economic problems.

Christopher Mason was President of the Cambridge University Liberal Club 1963–64. He has been a member of Strathclyde Regional Council since 1982 and was Chairman of the Scottish Liberal Party 1987–88. In April 1994 he was the first Liberal Democrat elected to the new unitary Glasgow City Council.

LORD MAYHEW

'We called a press conference, and I issued this statement.

The Labour Party has done immense service to the country over the years. I am proud to have belonged to it and fought for it since before the war, and feel sad at parting company with so many good colleagues in Woolwich and Westminster.

But as these colleagues know, I have for some years been very concerned at the way the party has been developing. In particular it has become too vulnerable to the extreme left and too dependent on the unions. Time and again in the past, moderate members, including myself, have tried to change this and to broaden the basis of the party, but with declining success, especially since Hugh Gaitskell's death. I can no longer feel genuinely convinced that a clear Labour majority at the next election will be in the country's best interest, so I have resigned.

Like other moderate Labour MPs, I have long shared many convictions with the Liberals, for example on Europe, east of Suez, industrial relations and the redistribution of wealth. But at the present time, I particularly support their campaign for political realignment. We need a revolt of the centre against the extremes. We must break away from the old Tory–Labour confrontation which sets one half of the country against the other. It is not impossible if enough people vote Liberal. I believe it will happen.'

– FROM 'TIME TO EXPLAIN', PUBLISHED IN 1987.

Christopher Mayhew was a Labour MP 1945–50 and 1951–74; he resigned the Labour Party to become a Liberal MP in 1974, was made a life peer in 1981 and is currently Lords spokesman on defence.

LORD MCNALLY

There is the old political joke about the Conservative candidate addressing an election rally who says: 'I was born a Conservative, I am a Conservative and I will die a Conservative'. A voice from the back shouts 'Man, have you *no* ambition?'. For many there is a certainty almost from the cradle about their political allegiance; the dyed in the wool socialist, the true blue Tory, the life long liberal. For other, more tormented souls, political life is more of an odyssey than a career path. We know what we believe. The task is to find a political home where personal conviction and party policy match.

In 1968, as a young Labour Party researcher I had the job of preparing a paper for the then deputy leader of the Party, George Brown. The paper required a definition of social democracy, and I wrote: 'Social democracy is not anti-communist or anti-capitalist. It is a philosophy in its own right which allows every individual to develop his or her own talents to the full; but also asks of every individual a commitment to ensuring all citizens a certain quality of life'. I repeat it now not because it is very profound; but because it captures the essence of what has always been at the heart of my personal politics: individual liberty – communal responsibility. In the

1980s both the intolerance of the Bennite Labour Party and the indifference of Thatcherite conservatism repelled me.

Unlike some (on both sides) who had been deeply involved in the 1976–78 Lib–Lab Pact, I did not find the experience uncomfortable or diluting of my true political purpose. On the contrary, I found it encouraging that politicians could work in partnership for the common good. It was that experience together with Bennite extremism in the Labour Party which led me first to the SDP and then, via merger, to the Liberal Democrats. I am often asked why, in the light of the Blair revolution and the creation of New Labour, I do not rejoin the Labour Party. It seems to me, however, that what is on offer from New Labour is a rather desiccated, managerial response to the challenge of the new right. New Labour does not suggest a new order of things – only a promise to try and run the old order a little better. In that respect I believe that New Labour fails the challenge of our time just as surely as do the Tories.

I am a Liberal Democrat because the Party does not shirk the linkage between public expenditure and social justice, equality of opportunity and quality of life.

I am a Liberal Democrat because the Party is genuinely committed to pluralism and the devolving and sharing of power in our grotesquely over-centralised state.

I am a Liberal Democrat because our commitment to work at the heart of Europe for the ever-closer union of the European peoples is the only realistic response to the old Dean Acheson jibe that Britain had lost an Empire and failed to find a role in the world.

I am a Liberal Democrat because through the Party I believe I can help create the political circumstances where the individual is more free, the community more strong, our society more tolerant and at ease with itself than would be the case without us.

Tom McNally is Head of Public Affairs at Shandwick Consultants. A Liberal Democrat peer since 1995, he was political adviser to the Prime Minister 1976–79, a Labour MP 1979–81, and an SDP MP 1981–83.

CATHERINE MILLAR

The most flippant answer would be that, as the daughter of a man who was named after the great Gladstone, I had little option. I must have breathed liberalism with my first breath and was certainly brought up in a household where there were often meetings, much political debate, gatherings of canvassers and leaflet deliverers. I remember stuffing acres of leaflets while trying to revise for my A-levels.

There comes a time when even the most brainwashed can step back and re-evaluate. This I did when I left home for university. I flirted briefly with the other parties displaying their wares to 'freshers', but it was a brilliant performance by Jo Grimond at the university union that confirmed liberalism for me as the political philosophy that I wanted for my own.

There have been many changes to the Party since Jo's day but the way has always been forward. Though sometimes I have felt disenchanted, often felt disenfranchised because the iniquitous voting system has deprived me of the chance to elect my chosen candidates, I have always been determined to stay with the Party and register, if nothing else, my vote for reason, justice, caring for others, civil liberty, democracy, and the grandest ideal of my lifetime – that of a united and peaceful Europe. And what I like most about the Party is that, not allied to the great battalions of big business or to a narrow doctrinaire class consciousness, it can truly represent independence of thought and respect and care for the individual. Perhaps the Party is not always pragmatic – but I like it for that, for its honesty and integrity and courage to promote what is sometimes unpopular because that is what is right.

Catherine Millar retired early from a Deputy Headship in Somerset, having taught in grammar, comprehensive and independent schools. She was a member of the arts policy working group.

CLLR ANN MOORE

Negative reasons, perhaps, at first sight: I was born a liberal, brought up a liberal, and have never seen another political philosophy which I preferred. My mother was a member of Lloyd George's Manchester staff in the 1920s and I am told I went to tea with him at the age of six weeks. Certainly 'LG' was a family icon in my childhood, only flawed when he accepted a peerage. My first political activity was to tell after school at a polling station in 1945, convinced the Liberals would form the next government ....

Why didn't I rebel, in a healthy teenage way? I certainly thought about it, tried to persuade myself there was something deficient in following in my parents' footsteps. The answer lies in the second part of my opening sentence: no other party has offered so congenial a spiritual or philosophical home. In this, for me, lies the essential difference between liberalism and other political ideologies – that it has a philosophical coherence, based on fundamental principles, which other parties lack, or if they have such a basis, as for example, true socialism, it is one I find fundamentally flawed.

John Stuart Mill expresses, for me, the essence of liberal philosophy, which is that responsibility, duty, and hence government, start within the conscience of each individual and move outward and upwards, as do needs and rights. So the individual's responsibility to answer the needs of the community should, equally, be expressed through the needs of other individuals, even if these can only be met collectively; rather than as the Marxist believes, starting with 'society' or the state and moving downwards. The application of these principles empirically (not pragmatically) to the infinite variety of the human condition produces a political system which is at least less imperfect than any of the alternatives.

Twenty-five years in local government (amid 16 years of Thatcherism) has only reinforced the validity of these concepts, and union with elements of the SDP has not diluted them.

Ann Moore assisted her husband, Richard Moore, in eight Westminster and one European elections. She has been a councillor on East Sussex County Council and/or Rother District Council (sometimes both) since 1973. Chair, Liberal Summer School.

SIMON MUNDY

When I was 20 there was no political party which I felt comfortable enough to join, so I stood for the student union as an independent. Slowly, though, it dawned on me that this was an absurd stance. In a democracy, however imperfect, that operated by giving power to groups of like-minded people (whether they be politicians or football administrators) to remain honestly independent can be a pure but futile pursuit. Either I had to find a party or I had to found one and the latter seemed much too much like hard work, not to say outrageously vain.

Politics had been a passion since my early teens, however, and I always loved the theatre of parliament. There is nothing wrong with that phrase. The Greeks held their great political debates in amphitheatres. There is no reason why debates should not be theatrical now. Wandering into the Strangers' Gallery (what an insult that term is to voters who want to watch their representatives) is a delight on a wet afternoon in London. On one such occasion in 1978 the Commons was dealing with one of Denis Healey's endless and increasingly desperate Finance Bills. On the Liberal bench sat John Pardoe and Alan Beith – not earnestly checking points of detail or snoring gently but shaking with laughter. Any party with a sense of humour in a moment of national crisis had the right appeal. When David Alton won his byelection the following May I dropped off the fence and joined.

The Liberals, albeit the oldest political party, felt like the only one able to think youthfully, unfettered by tired ideology. The Liberal Democrats still do, though there are moments when the experience of government at the district level has made some of the policies too orthodox for real innovation. But there are signs in all our attitudes – to Europe, education, cultural life and international relations – of thoughtful consideration winning the battle with gut reaction; fear or envy.

There is a point of political definition which explains why I shall stay with the Party now. Liberal Democracy can be summed up as the art (definitely an art) of making the society serve the individual. Socialism – even in the world of New Labour – is the science of making the individual work for society. Modern conservatism is the practice – there is little of art or science in it – of forcing individuals to work for themselves. The first is the only philosophy with a long term future; offering an ambition beyond the mundane and a humanist belief in the worth of everyman.

Simon Mundy is a writer, Director of the Utrecht Early Music Festival in the Netherlands, and Vice President of the European Forum for the Arts and Heritage. Formerly he was Director of the National Campaign for the Arts.

RABBI JULIA NEUBERGER

When I look at our society in Britain, and think about how we regard our young and our old, I am appalled by the fact that we have broken faith with both extremes, in age terms. We guaranteed care 'from cradle to grave' with the foundation of the NHS in 1948, yet in many ways we have broken that promise to precisely the people who were most dubious about it in the first place, those who are now very elderly. Liberal Democrats are prepared to look at some of the hard issues about paying for social and medical care, and to have a debate about them, including the need to be honest about inheritance, about costs of care as well as cure, and about the value of caring in the public, private, or voluntary sector.

When it comes to our young, equally we have been prepared to sit and watch youth unemployment, and the lack of real jobs despite so-called youth opportunities. Despite urgent need for work on infrastructure and on care of the elderly and disabled, no-one is really prepared to talk about asking our young to do some of these activities. Again, I am a Liberal Democrat because we are prepared to ask some of these questions, and are also prepared to see policies in social care go beyond one electoral cycle.

But lastly I am a Liberal Democrat because I believe that ordinary people usually know best what is good for them. Neither big business nor centrist, dirigiste, governmental authority can answer the wishes, the desires, and the strong beliefs of people in the country wherever they live. I believe that Liberal Democracy is one way of giving power to people, asserting their rights and their responsibilities, and encouraging them to take part in a genuinely participative democracy, instead of always leaving it to 'them' up there, wherever 'there' might be.

Julia Neuberger was a member of the SDP National Committee, 1982–88; Chair, Patients' Association, 1988–91; Chair, Camden & Islington Community Health Services NHS Trust, and Chancellor, University of Ulster, since 1993.

DICK NEWBY

I grew up in a mining district of West Yorkshire. As a teenager I developed a strong desire to help change society to make it easier for people to fulfil their potential; an opportunity denied many of my contemporaries. Given my background, the Labour Party seemed the natural vehicle for promoting this change and I was an active member of the Party for ten years, at university and subsequently in London. By the early 1980s however, inner London Labour was dominated by intolerant extremists and had almost completely lost touch with the people it claimed to represent.

It was therefore an easy transition from Labour to the SDP and an easy decision to leave the civil service to work for the Party from its inception in 1981.

In the aftermath of the 1983 election, I became increasingly convinced that there was no room for both the SDP and Liberal Parties and was an early advocate of a merger between them. I am sure that the merger was indeed the best course and the new party was and remains the right one for me because it has consistently represented the principles and policies which brought me into politics.

The Liberal Democrat approach – inclusive, decentralist within a strong European framework, pluralist – seems to me to be going with the grain of society. Old structures and hierarchies are no longer capable of responding to an increasingly critical electorate, and without change, disillusion with politics and with democracy will grow.

The Liberal Democrats, uniquely, genuinely support the kind of constitutional change which can bring politics closer to the people. They are also genuinely concerned about the development of the individual and about those longer term policies- eg the environment – which will have a critical influence on our ability to sustain a decent society in our overcrowded island.

By temperament, Liberal Democrats are independent-minded, often cussed, sometimes idiosyncratic. But they are infused with a determination to pursue the public good in the communities in which they practice their politics. I am happy to be one of their number.

Dick Newby was SDP National Secretary 1981–88 and is currently Deputy Chairman of the Party's general election campaign team.

EMMA NICHOLSON MP

Leaving the Conservative Party was an agonising decision. However, the present Government was too at variance with my concerns, principles, loyalties and convictions for me to remain with them. There had to be a clean break to firmly establish my commitment to a caring, competitive society, to Britain's future within and outside the European Union, to the restoration and respect of local government and constitutional reform.

Joining the Liberal Democrats was a real joy. I recognised that the Liberal Democrats was the only political party which truly represented and furthered these principles on which my political dynamics rest.

I wish to see a vitalised and dynamic society, providing compassion and help to those vulnerable elements and communities which, during 17 years of Conservative rule, have been subject to derision and ridicule from tawdry ministers advocating hypocrisy and prurience of the worst kind. I have long been concerned for the welfare of single mothers, who are all too often scapegoated for society's ills, along with the plight of women prisoners, generally, as well as in parturition.

A nation which has become so ill at ease with itself in turn has a damaging effect on the competitive strengths of our economy. Social ills have been aggravated by the failure of our country to develop the talents of an individual to the full. As a people we are less skilled and less well educated than we need to be in a world which values trained intelligence and flexibility more than ever before.

In the wake of my decision to take up the whip of the Liberal Democrats, a number of people wrote to me in protest arguing for the withdrawal of Britain from the European Union. This is a most mistaken perspective and one which the Government is approaching, influenced by the muddied judgement of opportune politicians. Britain has to be inside the Union if we are able to influence Europe's direction. All too often our bargaining position is reduced by the conflicting and confrontational noises from the Cabinet.

As you probably know, I have a strong interest in humanitarian concerns which stem from my work with the Save The Children Fund and now the AMAR Appeal for the Marsh Arabs of Southern Iraq. The Liberal Democrats have consistently taken on board the moral obligation to tackle poverty, oppression and hunger wherever they occur throughout the world. I am at home with every member of our Party in these great and crucial issues.

And lastly I am a Liberal Democrat because I passionately believe our adversarial approach to politics in this country is in drastic need of change. Reform is required in all comers of Westminster to rid our system of sleaze, political and financial. In joining the Liberal Democrats, I have found a group of MPs who, like myself, believe that public service is the reason for our election and that our commitment of that goal must guide our political and personal decisions.

Emma Nicholson has been MP for Devon West & Torridge since 1987. She was Vice Chairman of the Conservative Party, 1983–87. In 1995 she joined the Liberal Democrats, and is now overseas development spokesman.

BARRY NORMAN

What attracted me to the Lib Dems – as, before that, to the Social Democrats – is the Party's firm belief in proportional representation. It seems to me that if we are ever to introduce democracy to this country, PR is essential. Where, after all, is the democracy in a political system that keeps one party in office for 17 or 18 years with the support of considerably less than 50 per cent of the voters?

PR would be a moderating influence, and God knows a little moderation would not come amiss in our currently benighted land. For far too long now the majority of us have had to stand helplessly by while the Tories pursued a relentless campaign of national asset-stripping, selling off everything the country owned, from oil to gas, to the telephones and electricity and now the railways.

And what do we have to show for it, apart from an increase in the number of exceedingly wealthy Tories? Nothing at all. Do we have a sound industrial basis? No, we do not. We have a school system that educates 15 per cent of our children and is happy to allow the rest to rot. We have a National Health Service that cares more for the welfare of its managers than the patients. We have cardboard cities and beggars on the streets. We have people trapped by negative equity in homes which the

Government implored them to buy – if, that is, they are fortunate enough to have homes at all.

All that the cynical policy of privatisation has achieved is to buy several election victories for the Conservatives, with the attendant arrogance, complacency, sleaze and corruption that too long a spell in office invariably brings.

I don't suggest that PR would, by any means, be the answer to all our problems. But I'm convinced that under the kind of consensus government it would create Britain would be financially, morally and spiritually a great deal healthier than it is today.

Barry Norman is an author, journalist and broadcaster. He was presenter of BBC Radio Four's Today, *1974–76 and of BBC1's* Omnibus *in 1982; from 1973–81 and 1983 to the present he has been writer and presenter of BBC1's* Film *programme.*

ROSALIND OAKLEY

I remember clearly why I became a Liberal. It dawned on me at an early age that success in our society depends largely on whether you conform to expectations or not. I recall the anger I felt during my school years at the system's emphasis on honing academic ability, at the expense of virtually any other attribute. Where was the celebration of intrinsic human worth, the pursuit of each individual's potential? It seemed to be a case of fit the mould or be discarded.

I was inevitably drawn to liberalism's championing of the freedom of the individual in mind, body and spirit.

The liberalism to which I was attracted, though, is not just about selfish individualism. It stresses our interdependence and recognises individual freedom only flourishes where freedom is shared and upheld by others. That is why social justice is such an important part of the liberal agenda for me. As a liberal I take pride in the heritage of Lloyd George's People's Budget and old age pensions, and Beveridge's architecture of the welfare state. Poverty, like ignorance and conformity, enslave the individual and quash the potential that is present in us all.

Rosalind Oakley works in the disability movement, which is still seeking civil rights for disabled people.

LEMBIT ÖPIK

I joined the Liberal Democrats because I want to live in a society where one person can win without another having to lose.

My parents come from Eastern Europe. Many of my relatives were literally liquidated by the Soviet political system for daring to have an independent view that disagreed with the state. I was lucky to grow up in the relatively free world, in a home where argument and debate were encouraged. It shaped my moral and political beliefs.

So what am I working towards? For me, top priority is personal freedom to be who I am. Freedom from oppression, and freedom to progress. I joined the Lib Dems once I realised that this was the only political grouping in this country that really thinks that way too.

The character of the Party is unlike anything I've seen in the Conservatives or Labour. If the Liberal Democrats were a single person, I think s/he would be a serious, slightly verbose and very intense person, who fundamentally cares about the quality of life other people have, spends a great deal of time on public service, and drinks a little too much alcohol on Christmas Day. S/he would also spend a lot of time thinking about the brave new world ahead. This, above all else, keeps them going through hard times.

The policies generally reflect this commitment to the individual. Liberal Democrats are intolerant of selfishness and self-seeking opportunists. But no-one gets criticised for holding radical political views, however outlandish, if they don't violate the freedoms of others. We're also fairly honest about the *big* issues (for me, the environment, education, tax). I've started wondering if Labour even cares about these, let alone understands them.

The Party isn't perfect. We sometimes forget to advertise our achievements – and others get the credit for our ideas. And we sometimes debate policies without seeing the big context – so we've got the odd stupid policy. And even we have some members who see politics as a means to personal gain – and this is damaging. But the great majority are OK.

Personally, I can get depressed about the huge effort we have to put in to move forward electorally. But I also know that if the things we wanted to achieve were easy, somebody else, with less staying power and little principle, would be there already.

Those who've left to join the Labour Party of the 1990s have traded their vision for power. I'm an idealist, and you have to stay an idealist to make changes. It's the harder road to travel, but when you arrive you know you've made it easier for others to follow.

Politics, like life, is a question of maximising the opportunity. I wanted to maximise my chance to make the world more like the one I want to live in. And, in the final analysis, that's why I'm a Liberal Democrat.

Lembit Öpik was born in Northern Ireland, with Estonian parents; he is a city councillor in Newcastle-upon-Tyne; Northern Region Deputy Chair; member of the Federal Executive; Deputy Chair of the English Party.

MONROE PALMER

It was in 1963 working long hours as a chartered accountant – always bringing work home – that Susette said, 'don't you have anything else to do?' I said that I had always wanted to help the Liberal Party. So I contacted Party headquarters and the local representative came to see me. Little was I to know that this would change my whole life.

I became active because I knew that I agreed with Liberal philosophy. The politician I most admired was Jo Grimond.

With my practical involvement in Party politics I discovered community politics. I was able to help individuals and groups of people by knowing how the system worked and how to get an unresponsive bureaucracy to listen and to act. Eventually, and it took a long time, I became a local councillor in the London Borough of Barnet, and for eight years led the Liberal Democrat group there.

Almost by accident I stood for parliament. I was pressurised to put my name forward in 1979, but have stood in every general election since then.

What makes me so persistent or so crazy? It is the belief that only liberal philosophy can steer Britain and its people to a better society. A society where everyone shall have the opportunity to rise to their greatest potential. A society which prizes the freedom of the individual. A society which, quite simply, cares.

I'm afraid the Thatcher/Major years have fostered a sense of greed and selfishness. I'm not sure if I will ever succeed, but I must try to be part of the force committed to make Britain a better place for *all* its people.

Monroe Palmer OBE FCA, Lib Dem Group Leader Barnet Council 1986–94; National Treasurer Liberal Party and Parliamentary Party 1976–83, PPC for Hastings & Rye.

SIR PETER PARKER

The emergence of the Liberal Democrats had the redeeming appeal for me of a fresh start for old beliefs and new hopes. I see political democracy as the way to an optimum diffusion of power (not maximum, that would be chaos), opening opportunities and in the process rendering privilege, capitalist or collectivist, relatively harmless. The Liberal Democrat position offers a unifying challenge to the dilemma of this century: the left committed to the establishment of socialism, and the right to the protection of capitalism. And capitalism has survived triumphantly thanks to the fact that Keynesianism has provided a way of tampering with it in a mixed economy. Now, however, the new threat is the crudity of the modern conservatism, which seems to be too ready to accept an awful price in terms of social fragmentation and inequities. So what next? Not simply Whig and Tory alternatives, because the old style Tories are being wiped out. But the Whig tradition seems to be pulling itself together.

The present century began with some sharing of the priorities between an emerging Labour Party, trade union-driven, and the powerful old Liberal establishment. The century is ending with the old Labour Party reforming itself out of recognition almost, the old Tory Party usurped by Thatcherism and the Liberal Democrats focusing with clarity the potential in a fusion of two powerful traditions: the Liberal individual conscience and readiness for reform with Labour's traditional commitment to community.

Personally, I broke with regret from the Labour Party in the early '80s, at the end of my seven years with the railways. It was not my experience on the rails that turned my vote. I am a believer in public service, and it is the deterioration of the public service ideal in British public life that I find so arrogantly offensive in the new conservatism – and in particular with the railways, of course. The pell-mell privatisation, without sensible argument or business plan, is miserably incompetent (Labour and Conservative Parties actually had a bipartisan attitude to BR in my time – they both wished the railways well without willing the investment properly).

I went with the SDP, above all, because I felt the Labour Party was dominated by trade unions; it lacked an industrial policy and its deadpan complacency towards electoral reform was turgid. I voted SDP and shared the surge of hope in their first election. Then the disappointment in the Alliance when it shot itself in both feet. A new alignment of the Liberal Democrats made sense because it confirmed its policies in three key areas for me. First, a consistent resolve to the development of the new Europe. Second, a determination to tackle systematically the reform of our ramshackle constitution. Third, a concentration on education, 'one of the greatest and noblest designs that can be thought on', as Milton put it, 'and for want thereof this nation perishes'. And there is more to it than simple, clear policies – there is a feel about the Liberal Democrats, a freshness which is a relief. The political democracy in this country is turbulent but stale. The Liberal Democrats I found attractively open to new ideas, and alliances, I hope; the Party seems resolved without being ideological – and businesslike without reducing life to that cliché of the bottom line. There is more to the good society than can be crammed into the bottom line.

PS – or rather a flashback – October 1951, Bedford Town Hall. The last moments of the vote count for the national election: Soames, Conservative; Fredericks, Liberal; Parker, Labour. The Liberal and Labour candidates are prowling through the long tables of exhausted counters. It seemed we were both losing, my vote falling short of Soames by about the total of the Liberal vote. He said cheerfully he wished he'd known it was going to be such a close run thing. Had he known, he said, he would have urged his followers at eve of poll to throw in their lot with Labour ....

Sir Peter Parker is an industrialist and former chairman of British Rail; he is involved in business and the arts.

NICHOLAS PARSONS

I have supported the Liberal Party since my university days. I have always felt that a third party is a valuable counter-balance in the political arena, especially when you have two major parties in our country often evenly balanced in popularity. This can encourage negative voting at the expense of a third party, and can often temper any extremes that either of the two major groups might expound.

I have always believed in the fairness of the proportional representation system of voting. This would give the Liberal Democrats a far larger number of seats in parliament, which would also reflect their popularity in the country, and help to achieve the political balance referred to above.

Nicholas Parsons is an actor, comedian and presenter; someone with many different and individual achievements to his credit in the world of show business.

JO PHILLIPS

Nobody said life was fair – why should it be? Each and every one of us is different, born to live, work, love, play and die in different circumstances. The core of liberalism and Liberal Democracy has always been to me the unshakeable faith in the potential of every individual person and the unswerving commitment to liberty. Liberty is not the false equality created by uniformity and narrow horizons where the state is all-powerful. Liberty to me is about not just recognising but encouraging each and every member of society to play his or her part and fulfil their own potential regardless of age, gender, class, race or creed.

When I joined the Liberal Party twenty years ago, I was the mother of two small children, working as a volunteer helping adults to read and write, and later to make their own television programmes. I felt then that literacy is one key that unlocks a different and wider world; but it's the freeing of the human spirit to look further, reach higher and discover more that creates self-confidence, which in turn gives people faith in themselves. Only then do people begin to take control of their own lives, their own communities – to build and change things for themselves.

That, to me is what lies at the heart of Liberal Democracy.

Jo Phillips is a journalist and broadcaster. She was the Head of Paddy Ashdown's Westminster office 1994–95.

CLLR JENNY RANDERSON

During a school sixth form debate prior to the 1966 general election I realised I was neither a Tory nor a socialist and I began to look at liberalism. In London at that time Liberals were a rare breed. I have never wavered in my allegiance, although I did not join the Party until 1979, despite teaching politics in the intervening years.

During that time I refined my reasoning. Above all, as I became increasingly concerned with the environmental crisis, I admired Liberals for talking about the environment in their manifesto at a time when most politicians didn't know the meaning of the word. I admired them for talking of social justice for the individual when Tories were not interested in social justice and Labour were not interested in the individual.

I am now a Liberal Democrat because I was an enthusiastic supporter of the Alliance, which gave the Liberals a realism we perhaps lacked before. I remain impressed by the compassion and openness of mind shown by true Liberal Democrats. We are a thinking party, as Tony Blair has realised as he rushes to embrace some of our best ideas. Nevertheless, he cannot embrace our philosophy; he cannot embrace what makes us tick as Liberal Democrats. We are still the only party which has no reason to want to undermine the success of any one section of society but genuinely wants the best for all.

The Tory monopoly of government has undermined society, and there is international agreement that socialism has failed and nationalism is dangerous. I am tired of the politics which believes that Big Brother knows best, and confidently await the time when the people of Britain realise that they can be trusted to run their own lives.

Jenny Randerson is a lecturer at a tertiary college in Cardiff, leader of the Liberal Democrat group on Cardiff City Council and PPC for Cardiff Central; she was formerly Deputy President of the Welsh Liberal Democrats.

CLLR TIM RAZZALL

I am a Liberal by blood. My father fought parliamentary elections. My grandfather celebrated the 1906 landslide by rolling a blazing tar barrel down York High Street.

I am a liberal by upbringing – from my early years frightened by tales of evil Tory landlords evicting Liberal tenants from North Yorkshire farm cottages.

I am a Liberal Democrat through action. Twenty-one years as a Richmond councillor leaves me as convinced a practitioner of community politics now as when I was first elected. I believe campaigning Liberal Democrat councillors really do make a difference.

I am a Liberal Democrat by conviction. No other party combines a commitment to the market economy with an understanding of the proper role of government.

Most of all, I am a Liberal Democrat through the historical imperative of liberalism. A 19th century political philosophy based on an optimistic view of humanity, trust in ordinary people and dislike of the corporate state shines as brightly in 1995 as it did for Gladstone. 'Trust in the people, qualified by prudence' is as good a definition of the liberal spirit for me as it was for him over 100 years ago.

Tim Razzall is 52. The last Treasurer of the Liberal Party, he has been Treasurer of the Liberal Democrats since 1988. He was elected councillor for Mortlake ward, Richmond, in 1974 and has been Deputy Leader of Richmond Council since 1983. He is now Vice Chairman of the Association of Liberal Democrat Councillors, having been President 1991–95.

CLLR SHEILA RITCHIE

The only obvious home for liberals is in this party. The Liberal Party in the 1970s, when I first came across it, was a bit of a joke .... until you saw what Liberals did. Even before I became a party person, I voted for the Liberals because they were the ones who 'got things done'; or 'even came round in the snow'.

As a victim of community campaigning, I then went to help, and having got my man re-elected to the council, joined up in 1980.

I'm still in, because the last 15 years hasn't left a moment to contemplate leaving. Except, of course, for the merger period. As a 'yes, but' I thought long and hard about the horrible things the sogs did to my party, and two things made me stay in. Firstly, the Association of Liberal Democrat Councillors decided proactively to make the Party feel good about itself again, and involved me in some of that work.

Secondly, the alternative place to go, Meadowcroft's liberals, were so illiberal in their intolerance of the rest of us.

Liberalism is about creating a world big enough to hold all shades of opinion and attitude. It is the opposite of dogmatic and dictatorial. My 'mindless activism' is one way of making that world even bigger.

Sheila Ritchie is a solicitor, graduating in 1979. She is a councillor, Gordon District 1988–96; agent for Malcolm Bruce MP; member Liberal Party/Liberal Democrats and ALC/ALDC since 1980.

REV. ROGER ROBERTS

In 1945 I was a young schoolboy. It was the end of the war, and local cinemas showed on their newsreels the horrifying pictures of the opening of the Nazi concentration camps.

With many others I looked at these pictures with complete horror: the mountains of human skeletons and the shuffling figures of those who had survived the barbarity of the Holocaust. How was it possible for human beings to act in this way towards one another?

Having seen what could happen when people treated others like this, I determined to strive for a world in which every individual, without regard to colour, background, nationality, religion – or any difference at all – would be treated with dignity and respect.

This dream is shared by others who are not in liberal ranks but, for me, it is only amongst liberals and Liberal Democrats that this emphasis on the dignity and value of each individual is the top priority. Any form of racism or discrimination is abhorrent to us and totally rejected.

Roger Roberts is a life long liberal; he fought Conwy in 1979, '83, '87, and '92, has held many posts in the Party and is currently Federal Vice President.

EARL RUSSELL

I am a Liberal Democrat because I am a liberal, and I am a liberal because it is the only alternative to conservatism. If I look for one incident to sum it all up, I find it in my wife's life rather than mine. At the age of five, she was an unbeliever attending a convent school, and came across a Jewish girl, picked on because she was not Catholic, in tears because she was being made to eat her own shit. She marched up to the girls accused of doing this, and asked them whether it was true. They admitted it was. She said: 'I think this is wrong. If you agree, you'll stop it. If you don't, come with me now to tell Mother Superior why you don't.' They stopped.

It is all here: the gut hatred of oppression, Mill's crucial realisation that majority rule is no guarantee against oppression, the intuitive reliance on due process, and the awareness that authority may protect liberty as well as threatening it.

As far back as I remember, I assumed the purpose of politics was to fight injustice, poverty and oppression; what else could be worth all that sweat? That ruled out the Conservatives; the question was between Liberal and Labour. Labour understood that the state might protect liberty. The Conservatives understood the state might threaten it. The real skill of politics is deciding when state action protects liberty and when it threatens it. This was a task only the Liberals were even attempting. The state's threat to liberty can be controlled only if it is bound by a set of legal and constitutional rules, of which the requirement of due process is symbolic. Labour have no gut understanding of this: they judge constitutional rules according to whether they favour or hinder their party at the time in question. They have no sense of form. For Liberals that sense of form is intuitive.

Labour supposed that injustice could be prevented by changing the balance between classes. Injustice is not done to classes: it is done to individuals. No doubt it is done to more individuals in some classes than in others, but shifting the balance between classes only changes the victims. Since 1832, liberals have been attempting the more far-reaching task of reducing the inequalities of power. That is worth doing. That means that when we are in office, we must reduce our own power. The loudest cheer I have ever had from a Party audience was for saying: 'if we were in power, we would be just as bad as the others: we'd need control just as much.' I am proud of my party for that cheer.

In the 1950s, people used to claim that Labour was the heir of the Liberal Government of 1906. They could never make that claim good because they had a false vision. Socialism does not exist; it is a chimera. During the sixties, it became apparent that because Labour pretended to that vision in opposition, they had to be far more right wing in office than otherwise they would have been. They have never understood liberal ideals, and now they are not socialists, they have turned conservative, because they falsely believe conservatism is the only alternative to socialism. When I listen to Labour, I hear the voice of Jeremy Thorpe ringing in my ears: 'the Labour Party? They're the most reactionary institution in the country'. I am still learning how right he was, and that is why we are the only alternative to conservatism.

Conrad Russell has been Professor of British History at King's College, London, since 1990. He is Lords spokesman on social security and a member of the Federal Policy Committee.

LADY SEEAR

I am a Liberal Democrat because:

1. I had a remarkable history teacher at school who introduced me to the Liberal thinkers and statesmen of the nineteenth century.

2. I was in Germany when the Nazis made their first big electoral advance, and I watched them centralise everything in sight, destroying pluralism. This left me with the unshakable conviction that power must be spread as widely as possible.
3. For philosophical and religious reasons I believe we are all members one of another, whether we like it or not.

Nancy Seear was made a life peer in 1971. She was Leader of the Liberal peers 1984–88 and has been Deputy Leader of the Liberal Democrat peers since 1988.

MARGARET SHARP

I believe passionately that we need to create in Britain, in the words of the preamble to the Party's constitution, 'a fair, free and open society' based on 'the fundamental values of liberty, equality and community, and in which no-one shall be enslaved by poverty, ignorance or conformity.'

In my view, the Conservative policies of the last 15 years have taken us in wholly the wrong direction. We have seen civil liberties curtailed; the Beveridge evils of ignorance, idleness, illness and poverty return to stalk our streets; and we have lost the concept of community to the promotion of selfishness and greed. Perhaps most dangerous of all, people are disillusioned and alienated from politics.

Investment and education are of course essentials. But where we Liberal Democrats are different is that we are the only party dedicated to changing not just the government, but the system of government. I believe we have now got to go back to the beginning and find ways of renewing people's trust in politicians and faith in the political process. This is why our principles of participation, cooperation and partnership are so important; why we need fair votes, open government and a written constitution; and why we need to see the powers and dignity of local democracy restored to local government.

Liberty, equality, community. These are my fundamental values and I positively want to stand up and be counted for adhering to them.

Margaret Sharp is a senior fellow at the Science Policy Research Unit, University of Sussex, a member of the Federal Policy Committee and PPC for Guildford.

CLLR ALAN SHERWELL

Socially the political system must provide opportunities for all individuals to achieve their potential and support to those who cannot, for whatever reason, provide fully for themselves. This involves combating discrimination and disadvantage but also implies that people must have the right to decide that they do not wish to achieve all of which they are capable.

Economically the political system must provide the resources for those social objectives to be met for this and succeeding generations. It must provide fair reward for endeavour, skill and ability and a safety net for those who need it.

Generally the system must give individuals a stake in society and confidence that improvement both personally and collectively is both possible and will proceed by consent.

Only a philosophy based on social liberalism and democracy can achieve this. Arguably conservatism is not a political philosophy at all. Certainly, if it means preservation of the social status quo, it is not possible in a changing world and, if it means preservation of the economic status quo and one-sided support for business, then it cannot provide security for the future or hope for the under-privileged in the present. Socialism, even if it can provide for the economic needs of the individual (and there is precious little evidence that it can), cannot provide for their social needs.

Only a liberal and democratic programme can provide equality of opportunity and the chance for individual and corporate progress by consent, whilst ensuring that effective support is given to those who need it.

Cllr Alan Sherwell joined the Liberal Party in 1967 at the age of 17, has chaired the National League of Young Liberals and been Vice Chair of the Liberal Party Policy Committee and National Executive. He is in his fifth year as Chair of the Federal Conference Committee and is Deputy Leader of Aylesbury Vale District Council.

ELIZABETH SIDNEY

A charismatic third yearer recruited me into the Oxford Liberal Party. When the stardust settled and I read the different parties' manifestos, I fortunately found myself happy to stay. I believed and still believe that society works best if people are free to develop their abilities and that the job of government is to promote and protect that freedom.

Political adherence is an informing faith. Professionally, I have worked for democracy in the workplace and for personnel practices which give greater equality of opportunity. Politically, I have worked mainly for equality for women. Not only are they the most obviously disadvantaged group in our partial democracy but their emancipation must mean emancipation for all.

As a Liberal Democrat, I am a paid up Europhile. It is crazy not to integrate with and learn from the culturally richest corner of the globe. Additionally, environmental protection, health, education, transport, sustainable economics all impel us towards integration. Of course, the European institutions must be drastically reformed and democratised; hopefully the 1996 Inter-Governmental Conference will move us on.

Constitutional reform of the UK is equally crucial; Charter 88 is of course a Liberal stronghold.

For the present, Liberal Democrats seek political power with little hope of attaining it. One can be altruistic, but not happy, to watch our policies being regularly plundered. I carry on because we embrace diversity, and I believe an egalitarian society is the only type which can survive long term. And the continuing existence of a third party, however lamentably under-represented, is a lasting challenge to the crude domination produced by a two-party system. For the future, I look to constitutional reform and to the Internet; it could bring us transparency despite Conservatives, multinationals and Rupert Murdoch.

Elizabeth Sidney is managing consultant, the Mantra Consultancy Group; a former President, Women's Liberal Federation and European Liberals & Democrats; Executive, Women's National Commission.

ADRIAN SLADE

My two word answer would be Jo Grimond.

Jo's Liberal Party looked like the only political alternative for those of us from a fifties generation that had alternately laughed or despaired at Toryism, saw nothing very radical in Gaitskellism and sensed a great deal too much conservatism in the old Labour Party. When we woke up to politics, Jo was the only identifiable voice of real change.

Alone among political leaders, he seemed capable of undermining the system of the day. Who better to do so than an Old Etonian who knew it from within? His liberalism was about breaking down barriers at every level – a belief in an open and united Europe that went way beyond commercial opportunism, a commitment to a non-sectional partnership in the workplace that the other two parties could not dare to espouse because of their paymasters, and an internationalism and concern for human rights that no-one else was expressing at the time.

He was also the supreme iconoclast, with scant regard for the old boy network, the House of Lords, titles or the closed shop – 'traditions' as they were more often known in those days. He castigated the Tories' East of Suez imperialism and their continuation of the independent deterrent (a lesson for today?). He mocked puffery, pomposity and restrictive practices, particularly among his former colleagues at the Bar.

As an ex-Cambridge Footlight from a predominantly legal family background, I felt immediately at home with this man and his philosophy.

But Jo tempered idealism with realism. He preached realignment of the left and the creation of a non-socialist radical alternative to Toryism. It seemed the only logical way forward under the system of the day. I responded to it, and that is why, despite some initial hesitation about the birth of the Alliance and the traumas of the merger negotiations, I later welcomed the formation of the Liberal Democrats as the best hope for any fundamental change.

As the Tories move further back to the right, and Blair's Labour Party takes on the mantle of Harold Wilson, the old Jo messages still sustain me. For all the frustrations there is still no other party to which any self-styled progressive can possibly belong. Let us hope that the scent of power does not trim our radicalism beyond recognition.

Adrian Slade, the last Liberal President before merger with the SDP in 1988, advised the Party on publicity in 1966, '74 and '79 when he was also chairing the Publications Committee. A parliamentary candidate in 1966, '74 and '87, he was elected to the GLC in 1981 and led the GLC Alliance group until abolition. He remains politically active for the Liberal Democrats.

SIR CYRIL SMITH

I'm a person with a natural rebellious streak! No other party would contain me. Why? Because I am *not* a toer of party lines and dictates, and I demand the right to my own opinion and to express it.

I respect the right of other people to do likewise. Liberalism stands for the liberty of the individual, always provided that liberty does not interfere with the right of any other individual. It does not mean license – it does mean individual liberty. It means standing up and being counted. It means standing up for the little man against Big Brother bureaucracy. Liberalism is compassionate, caring and is concerned about *people*. It believes in people controlling their own destiny within an ordered society. It believes in equal opportunity.

It's because I believe in these values and principles that I am a Liberal Democrat.

Sir Cyril Smith MBE was the Mayor of Rochdale 1966–67; MP for Rochdale 1972–92; Liberal Chief Whip 1975–76.

MICHAEL STEED

The Liberal Party I joined nearly forty years ago was, under Jo Grimond's leadership, committed to realignment of the left. As I explored my Party's history, I realised how its appeal and endurance grew out of the decentralised, individualistic and ultimately rather chaotic way it came into being in the nineteenth century. How tragic it was for progressive politics in this century that such a pluralistic party was displaced as the opposition to the Tories by a party of stiflingly centralised collectivism.

Admittedly, as part of growing up, I went through a brief socialist phase. But the conviction of my late teens, that liberalism, not socialism, must be at the core of a worthwhile and effective radical party, has been triumphantly vindicated. Whatever 'New Labour' may turn out to be, everything it says about itself proclaims that a profound mistake was made a century ago by those on the left who insisted on setting up a new party based on class and socialist doctrine. I was one of those who did not find the actual transition from Liberal Party to Liberal Democrats easy; the merger process was made avoidably painful. But as a Grimondite Liberal, I never had any doubt as to the principle of merger with the SDP. I am a Liberal Democrat today in the hope of some further realignment.

My initial appreciation of liberalism derived from an early interest in nineteenth century history; Morley's *Gladstone* was one of the first 'adult' books I read. I came to believe in the Gladstonian mission to preserve peace rather than the Disraelian mission to extend the British Empire by force or fraud, in constitutional reform rather than the Tory defence of privilege, in freeing the economy to encourage enterprise rather than protectionism, in the rights of nations rather than those of hereditary rulers, and generally in the classic liberal search for principle and rationality as the basis for policy, rather than Conservative pragmatism.

This historical perspective might not have seemed relevant to a choice of political allegiance by a teenager born in 1940, but for a dramatic event and an enduring great issue.

First, Eden's armed attack on Egypt in 1956; the Suez affair confirmed all I disliked most about the instincts of the Conservative Party, while the total failure of the British parliament to hold anyone accountable for this war crime (contrast the effectiveness of parliament a century earlier over the Crimean War) exposed the hypocrisy and superficiality of the much-vaunted merits of Westminster democracy. Suez and Tory imperialism have faded into history, but the aggressiveness of the Tory right (witness Portillo's following) and the impotence of parliament remain dominant features of the British political landscape.

Next, my imagination was stirred by the essentially Cobdenite ideal of ensuring lasting peace through European integration. On this issue Labour was easily the most reactionary and protectionist party; the pragmatic Tories were actually more progressive than Labour, and were to remain so until the 1990s! But pragmatism kept us out of the European Communities in 1958. This failure, and the carping, negative role inside which both Labour and Tory governments have played since 1974, set this country back enormously.

Throughout my political life, the Liberal Party has been consistent, forward-looking and positive about Europe; that alone justified my choice, even through it effectively ruled out a political career. It is a tragedy that the configuration of the party system on this issue, combined with the undemocratic voting system, has excluded from parliament and from political office so many who have understood why Britain's interests lie in Europe.

Many other issues have confirmed my Liberal allegiance. If I had been born in 1950, it might have been the Party's anti-Vietnam War stance or its anti-racism which first attracted me; if in 1960 perhaps its distinctively green policies or its courage over gay rights; if in 1970 probably constitutional reform and Europe again.

My reflection in semi-retirement is that liberalism has a better understanding of economics, and of the limited role of government in the economic field than socialism or traditional conservatism; of the complexity of human nature; of the human need for freedom in which to find fulfilment; and perhaps most of all of the importance of getting the institutional framework for human society right. One of the best snap definitions of a liberal is 'someone who combines emotional anarchism with intellectual constitutionalism'.

Michael Steed was born into a Conservative farming family, went to Cambridge University, became Chairman of the Union of Liberal Students in 1962 and President of the Liberal Party in 1978. He is now an honorary lecturer in politics at the University of Kent at Canterbury.

DENIS SULLIVAN

Conversion, tenacity and tolerance:
the life-sustaining forces of a political nobody

I discovered by the age of fifteen that politicians could change the lives of ordinary people. A local councillor who I had canvassed for was instrumental in having slums condemned. That experience of being near to power, and its working for the common good, had a profound, long-lasting impact.

As a result of that experience I spent a lifetime pursuing a career as a failed politician.

Naturally I regret my lack of personal success, but the feeling of having contributed in a small way to social improvement has sustained me even in difficult times of single percentage polls.

But there have been moments: the decision of the Scottish Constitutional Convention to adopt PR as its electoral system proves that perseverance pays dividends.

I never imagined that when I embarked on a life in politics it would be such a roller-coaster, nor did I realise that my own views would change and alter on the anvil of experience. It has taught me that the greatest political virtue of them all is tolerance.

Denis Robertson Sullivan is now a political lobbyist and Treasurer of the Scottish Liberal Democrats. He has spent a lifetime standing and not being elected and doing every conceivable job the party(s) have asked, including dressing as a dragon during Roy Jenkins' Hillhead byelection victory – proud he is not.

DR GLYN TEGAI HUGHES

No Damascene conversion took place; from an early age liberalism had seeped into my bones, courtesy of a highly selective version of Welsh nineteenth century history. I never had a moment's doubt that the Tories were repressive landlords, bigoted churchmen, hard-faced financiers, brewers' puppets, and general face-grinders of the poor. A good number of public school products at Cambridge did little to modify these views, amply confirmed, of course, by the present Government.

Labour was less unappealing, but not by much. One wanted to believe that its heart was in the right place, but it housed so many crabbed zealots and unattractive bullies that such a leap of faith was impossible. And how could anyone believe that some single system from the detritus of nineteenth century philosophy (in this case Marxism, but one might well later say the same of monetarism) could address the complexities of society?

A Welsh speaker will have some emotional tug towards Plaid Cymru and will not relish being thought an Uncle Tom for not following it. The package, however, is too constricting, its sympathies too narrow; I could never really find the Basques as interesting, let alone relevant, as the English. Its European instincts are by now more highly developed, the doctrines of appalling interwar French thinkers long since abandoned; but the vision still seems anaemic and unreal.

These negative reasons are merely a confirmation of the positive appeal of liberalism. The Liberal Democrat party is as undogmatic, as wide-ranging in its search for solutions, as firmly rooted in a civilised view of society and as free of external pressures as a political party can reasonably be; as such it can react swiftly to changing social, economic and intellectual patterns. It is a deeply depressing feature of much contemporary infighting that this ability to change stance can be regarded as weakness.

Glyn Tegai Hughes was formerly a Liberal candidate, Governor of the BBC, and Warden of Gregynog, University of Wales.

SIR MALDWYN THOMAS

I was born a liberal! That is to say, I grew up in a liberal family. My earliest recollection of political activity is delivering election leaflets in Rhondda East, as a schoolboy, for the Liberal candidate in the late 1920s. To deliver political leaflets in that emotive, politically charged environment was fairly foolhardy!

That youthful activity bred an instinctive loyalty to the Liberal Party but not, in itself, the conviction and understanding of the tenets of liberalism which I came to recognise and accept over the years that followed.

The more I thought about liberal philosophy, the less I was attracted to socialism, which seemed a depressing doctrinal straitjacket, and conservatism, which, in general, came over as expedient, short-term, and sectionally motivated. These perceptions are, of course, intellectually superficial, because little in life is either totally black or white. I am attempting to describe the way in which a young mind reacted over the years to the competing mainstream politics on offer.

During my candidature as a Liberal in the 1950 general election, I recall enthusing about the 'golden thread of consistency' running through Liberal policy stemming from the freedom of the individual, social fairness and compassion, and the nurturing of democratic institutions.

The years have gone by, but I am even more persuaded that the golden thread does exist and does apply in the evolution of liberal attitudes enshrined in the philosophy of the Liberal Democrats. It seems to me that is both a coherent concept and a guide to measuring the 'quality' of political solutions.

Sir Maldwyn Thomas was President of the Welsh Liberal Party. A non-practising barrister, he became Chairman & Chief Executive of Rank Xerox, and a director of Xerox Corp. USA.

CLLR JOHN TILLEY

It might be more impressive to claim some great intellectual reasoning for being a liberal. That would be nothing more than a pose. I am a liberal because I put freedom first, because I want to change the world. I am a 'Liberal Democrat' because that is for the time being the name of the political party to which most liberals belong.

It is probably also equally true that I am a liberal because my beliefs have been shaped and underlined by my background and experiences in life. Born in Wythenshawe (South Manchester) in the 1950s, in a council estate like hundreds of others, I doubt if many people would have spotted a future liberal leader of the Royal Borough of Kingston upon Thames.

I grew up in a working class family with few books, few pretensions – but with the advantage of intelligent parents who had more common sense and ability than society would ever have given credit for.

We did, however, have a TV; I am probably one of the first generation in the UK unable to remember a time without television. My father watched the news and *Panorama* and he usually had a view (probably not often liberal). From an early age I watched with him. In the 1960s the TV news was full of the USA, civil rights marches, Martin Luther King. The non-news programmes, the westerns, Perry Mason, *Ready Steady Go,* were sometimes somehow even more 'political' than the news.

I am a liberal because of the views I formed at that time. I saw the world via the BBC, ITV and Hollywood. Films like *To Kill a Mocking Bird, The Man Who Shot Liberty Valence, A Taste of Honey, Room at the Top, In the Heat of the Night* and *The Great Escape* all influenced me. All seen in black and white on TV and all seen years after they were made. James Stewart, John Lennon, Martin Luther King, Jo Grimond and John Arlott. TV gave me a great jumble sale of characters and ideas from which I picked the ones I liked best. We did not read weighty political books, but we did watch TV.

So when in the late 1960s and early 1970s I started to hear about people like Peter Hain (heard him first because he was on TV), Tony Greaves and Gordon Lishman, the things they said fitted in with the view I had already formed. Freedom was good. Injustice was bad. Apartheid was evil, Martin Luther King was right, passive resistance, non-violent action was the way to break the system. The Vietnam War was wrong – young people, peace and love were right. Nixon was bad, Wilson was a fool or worse, Labour had sold us out.

It became obvious that TV politics were not good enough. We had to stop being watchers and start doing something. John Lennon put out the record *Power to the People.* I thought I would give it a try. The Young Liberals talked about taking power and using it. That's why I am a liberal. I believe that politics should be about working with people to take power and use it.

John Tilley is Leader of Kingston Council, which successfully devolved power to Neighbourhood Committees. Positively anti-Labour. Liberal, republican, likes gardening and heckling.

LORD TORDOFF

I was brought up, both in my family and at school, in an atmosphere where one was taught to value people more than possessions; in an ethos that regarded self-discipline as the most effective control on human actions, either individually or as a community. Hence liberty was to be regarded as a positive force for general happiness, and respect for the well-being of others the major constraint on the exercise of that liberty.

This did not bring me into active politics (save only for being the sole Liberal in the 'parliament' of the Middle School Debating Society in the early 1940s) until Suez. I had been attracted by the Liberal Party's commitment to worker participation for some time and had voted Liberal whenever I had the chance, which was not all that often in those days. Although not having the courage to be a pacifist, I had come to the conclusion at the end of the war that it was not an acceptable way of solving international disputes and that the United Nations had to be the way forward. Now Britain decided that the Suez Crisis had to be settled by force of arms. I felt betrayed, and could only see Jo Grimond and the Liberal Party having the courage to stand out against sabre-rattlers. When I found that there wasn't a Liberal candidate in my constituency at the next election I joined soon after.

The things which are central to my political feelings and beliefs are, I suppose, a hatred of concentrations of power and consequently of class distinctions, inherited wealth, state centralism, racism and intolerance of all kinds.

I suppose, when I think about it, the preamble to the Party's constitution pretty well says it all.

Geoffrey Tordoff was born in 1928; Liberal candidate Northwich 1964, Knutsford 1966 and '70; former Party Chairman and President. He was made a life peer in 1981 and was Lib/Lib Dem Chief Whip in Lords 1984–94. He has been Principal Deputy Chairman of House of Lords Committees since 1994.

CLLR MIKE TUFFREY

I can explain it rationally. But the truth lies deeper, with emotions and instinct, upbringing and family background. At the superficial level, one reason why I am a Liberal Democrat is policy: decentralisation, empowerment, involvement, local, people, and all those other words from the liberal lexicon. (And why I remain is, in all honesty, partly because I have won the rare opportunity to enjoy the real stuff of political power. Running an organisation spending £600 million a year, employing 12,000 people and having enormous influence, good and bad, on the lives of some of Britain's most disadvantaged citizens, is immensely satisfying.)

But the real reasons go deeper, beyond the here-and-now. Some of my family roots grow in Quaker nonconformity. My grandfather ended up a prosperous businessman and local Liberal worthy. That, plus growing up in Orpington in the sixties and early seventies, meant third party politics was not totally implausible. My formative political years were under Ted Heath's 1970–74 Government, followed by the insipidity of Wilson/Callaghan. Today I still find little that inspires in Major and Blair. Instinctively too, I recoil from divisions in society – the two sides of industry, the two-party duopoly, the haves versus the have-nots – and something in my psyche makes me seek cooperation, not confrontation.

In short, part policy, part patrimony, part personality.

Mike Tuffrey shares the leadership of Lambeth Council, having led the Lib Dem group since 1990, now the equal largest party. He was first elected to the GLC-ILEA in 1985, as the then youngest member, and has stood for parliament three times.

PAUL TYLER MP

I decided I was a liberal the night in October 1956 when Eden's Government authorised the RAF to bomb Egyptian towns along the Suez Canal. It was a case of 'stop the world, I want to get on'.

Subsequently, I became a Grimond disciple. Although by upbringing an Anglican – and convinced that toleration, pluralism and personal liberty are all Christian values we should carry into public life – I became increasingly non-conformist in politics. That may be a strange ancestral mix: Cromwell via my father mitigating the effect of Bishop John Trelawny, the Cornish folk hero, from my mother.

I suspect that if we had a Liberal Democrat government, conformity would still be my anathema. The underdog may not always be right, but his or her view deserves a hearing. Even the minority who want to make scapegoats of another minority are better dealt with by rational debate than by dictatorial suppression which gives them martyrdom status. Thus, electoral reform is not just about achieving elusive 'fairness' but about creating mechanisms for a mature democracy.

It is nearly 40 years since I decided I could never be a Conservative, rooted in the narrow nationalism and class snobbery of the last century. Seeing now at close quarters the Parliamentary Labour Party in all its tribal exclusivity – Blair or no Blair – it seems an equally unsuitable vehicle for the pluralist politics of the next century. The challenges of post-cold war fission make both look dangerously introvert.

The Liberal Democrats may not be perfect, but we have our uses.

Paul Tyler has been MP for North Cornwall since 1992, and is rural affairs spokesman. He was Party Chairman, 1983–86, and a general election coordinator in 1983 and 1987.

RICHARD WAINWRIGHT

By accident I had two Liberal school teachers; and university tuition in political theory convinced me that a liberal polity would be the best form of government. Furthermore, Keynes – a declared Liberal – had been giving the Party dynamic policies for the stagnant economy and mass unemployment.

At a much lower level, from the precarious platform of the University Liberal Club I did battle with aggressive meritocrats – an illiberal species still to be found in universities, and even in sixth forms.

At that time I came upon the sharpest liberal armament to carry through life: 'the poorest he that is in England hath a life to live as the greatest he' – Thomas Rainborowe, of Cromwell's army; not a life prescribed or imposed by others, but his own life which only he can live.

Buttressing this, for me, was and is the Quaker belief: 'there is that of God in every man and woman'.

Came World War Two, with liberalism one of its sorest casualties. Labour and Tory alike fostered the fallacy that because huge central planning prevailed in the narrow focus of war, with personal lifestyles willingly put aside, it would equally 'win the peace' despite the myriad differences of peacetime aspirations and the vast expansion of services and products. Businesses already made huge by war were deliberately enabled to grow bigger still, and likewise trade unions. It became ever clearer that liberalism was not central between the other two parties, but way out ahead with a thoroughly distinct agenda. A key part of that postwar agenda was William Beveridge's *Full Employment in a Free Society* – still my basic text when Jo Grimond, in 1966, made me spokesman on the economy.

To fight elections *to win* called for truly distinctive Liberal policies, sharply relevant to Britain's long-term problems – way ahead of Butskellism and the concealed two-party consensus. Jo Grimond's quiverful of reforming ideas met this need, especially his inspired embrace of the Treaty of Rome. As early as 1956 his party of six MPs was the lone advocate of Britain being a founder member of the EEC.

All this led me in 1957 to start fighting to represent Colne Valley – a traditionally Labour seat. It then comprised some thirty industrial communities, each with its local woollen mills and maybe a smallish engineering plant. There were no traces of high society, but a great buzz of voluntary groups and clubs, deeply rooted and taken seriously. Amongst these folk and their five urban district councils I found that liberalism actually works, and animates some deeply and widely held beliefs.

One lesson I soon learnt was the folly of trying to impose sound Liberal measures (comprehensive schools, for instance) by illiberal centralised government power – as Labour did in the seventies: though that view was not, alas, held by all Liberal MPs.

By the end of seventeen years in the Commons I saw clearly that it is not only political fairness and honesty which should motivate thorough constitutional reform, but also the crucial business of making democratic government effective and making acts of parliament stick.

I have nowhere used the term 'radical'. When Thatcher got going I spewed it out of my vocabulary. I don't intend to put it back.

Richard Wainwright was formerly President, Cambridge University Liberal Club; Chairman, Yorkshire Liberal Federation; Liberal MP, Colne Valley, 1966–70 and 1974–87 (stood down at age 70); spokesman on the economy, 1966–70 and 1979–85.

MIKE WALLACE

I joined the Young Liberals to meet people. My parents had been Liberals for many years, and I had helped in elections, but that was enthusiasm for action and to be involved rather than an interest in politics itself. Putney Young Liberals was different. Apart from enjoying meeting each other, we discussed current political issues, and looked for ways of changing the world. We were clearly young and idealist. Non-violent direct action really inspired us. It was the era of the 'Stop the Seventy Tour' (the South African cricket tour planned for the UK), of food boycotts, of 'Don't play with Apartheid' stickers. We were also inspired by the writings and speeches of Jo Grimond. Here was a man of vision, someone with ideas that we could follow and share.

It was through that background that several of us became officers of the South East Young Liberal Federation. We wrote and published a booklet setting out our thoughts and feelings for the Liberal Assembly in Brighton. Then we moved on to the National League of Young Liberals. Peter Hain became Chairman. Graham Tope and Gordon Lishman were also national officers with me. It was at this time that a real interest in politics grew.

Leaving the NLYL, I found myself having no local political connections in Sussex where I had moved to. It was 1973. New district councils were being set up and the first elections were to be held. I stood – with little real expectation of success, but it kept me involved.

To everyone's surprise, I was elected in a ward which had previously been a Tory stronghold. Lots of enthusiasm and Focus leaflets had worked. I stayed on the Mid-Sussex District Council for 14 years, always in opposition, but able to achieve some things. Mainly helping individuals, sometimes even persuading the Tories to change their policies. But I saw the way that power was not so slowly been eroded from local government to Whitehall – and how individual authorities could do little to oppose – especially if they were Tory and did not want to!

My job meant I could not continue on the council in 1987 so I did not stand for reelection, but my interest remained then and now. I still have a desire to try to make the world a better place, where people count more than institutions; where there is freedom but it is always tempered by a sense of responsibility willingly accepted by all; where there is genuine equality of opportunity; where there is control on the ability of corporations and institutions to exploit their power. I want to see a just and fair society, with a sense of community. A society where people are willing to be involved and committed not for personal gain, but for the benefit of all.

We have lost a generosity of spirit which we need to regain. I want greater understanding and tolerance at all levels of the society and world in which we live. It is in the Liberal Democrats that I think the greatest hope exists to achieve these.

Mike Wallace has held various posts in the Liberals and Liberal Democrats at national, regional, constituency and local level. Currently President, Mid Sussex Liberal Democrats and Managing Director of the UK subsidiary of an international German company.

LORD WALLACE

Liberalism isn't a matter of revealed truth or doctrine: commitment comes from a long learning process, reinforced by experience. I didn't come from a political household – though my father would lecture me on social equality as we cycled to visit the local farmers and gentry who held accounts in his branch of Barclays Bank. The first political speeches I heard were Anglican sermons: Canon Marriott preaching on justice and community to a crowded Westminster Abbey when I was a chorister, John Habgood and Alec Vidler later in Cambridge churches and chapels. Suez and Hungary, erupting together when I was fifteen, threw me into passionate school debates, shaking the passive conservatism of a middle-class teenager.

Arriving at university with an unfocused interest in politics, I joined all three main political clubs. Conservative snobbery and social climbing, doctrinal conflicts among the factions of the Labour Club, combined with discovery of John Stuart Mill, TH Green, Hobhouse and the more recent writings of Donald Wade and Elliott Dodds to make me a conscious and active Liberal. Studying nineteenth century English history alongside observation of contemporary British politics convinced me of the case for constitutional reform. And then there was Jo Grimond: articulate, idealistic, persuading his audiences that politics could be about something more than class advantage or personal gain, arguing that Britain would continue to drift into post-imperial decline unless it renewed its political institutions, abandoned the romantic commitment to world status and a 'special relationship' with the United States, and came to terms with its European partners.

It wasn't easy to remain a political Liberal after the exhilaration of the first, 1960s, revival subsided. Politics, as Hugh Gaitskell had argued, is a necessary compromise between idealism and practical possibilities. Given the political impotence of the Liberal Party after Labour's decisive victory in the 1966 general election, the retirement of Grimond, and the recovery of the Conservatives to regain power in the 1970 election, it was tempting to try to pursue the ideals of social liberalism through the Labour Party and its social democratic wing. Harold Wilson's sharp shift towards Euro-scepticism in 1971–72, reinforced by acquaintance with the patronising style and petty corruption of the Manchester City Labour Party, cured me of that temptation. During the 1975 referendum campaign I first worked with some of those I got to know later as Social Democrats in the Alliance, speaking in the north-west on platforms where Labour MPs were arguing opposing European cases.

A less class-ridden Britain, politically renewed through constitutional reform, economically revived through employer-employee cooperation and through integration with continental Europe: these were the ideas, half-articulated at first, that moved me into politics and kept me active over the years. Other convictions have clustered around them. Reading through the debates on Irish Home Rule, as a history student, planted a distaste for English nationalism and the mythology of parliamentary sovereignty which has grown with every Europhobe speech and every downgrading of local government at the expense of this centralising doctrine.

Part of that mythology is that Britons are naturally free, not needing the entrenched protection of political and civil rights which lesser states require; the complacent disregard for individual liberties which accompanied such beliefs taught me the importance of strengthening the rights of citizens against the state. Political activity over 30 years, first in Huddersfield, then in Manchester and Bradford, then bringing up our children in south-west London, has taught me a lot about the threat of racism and the value of building a multiracial society. The shattering of established local communities by Labour authorities through compulsory purchase, wholesale demolition and rehousing, painfully observed in Huddersfield and Manchester, had shown me the importance of community and of local participation well before the economic liberals launched their attack on the concept of society as such.

Why am I a Liberal Democrat? From experience and from conviction, and from the interaction between experience and conviction. I see the Party as continuing to represent the social liberal tradition in British politics, as inherited from Gladstone and Mill, Keynes and Beveridge, Grimond and Wade and others. Traditions and beliefs need continual reinterpretation to fit changing circumstances, however. Post-Thatcherite British politics, with its unhappy mixture of negative nationalism, widening inequalities, social insecurity and popular disillusion with political democracy, presents us with the difficult task of persuading a sceptical electorate that the principles of social liberalism offer the best way forward.

William Wallace (Lord Wallace of Saltaire) was appointed a Liberal Democrat working peer in 1995. He fought five parliamentary elections as a Liberal between 1970 and 1987, was a member of the Party's Standing Committee (now Policy Committee) 1975–89, and of the Alliance Joint Leaders' Committee 1983–86.

CLLR DIANA WALLIS

I grew up in a Labour-voting household, indeed my mother had been a local Labour councillor on Watford Borough Council. When I first started to vote, therefore, it was for Labour. My mother had introduced me to some Liberal ideas which seemed to me good sense: employee share ownership, regionalism and, of course, PR.

However, although the Liberal candidate in Watford was 'such a nice man' – he always lost; it was a wasted vote, wasn't it?

Then came the referendum on Europe. As a teenager I was ardently 'European'. When it came to the vote, instinctively I wanted to vote for Europe, which represented what I really felt was our future, but conversely if I were a real socialist then I ought to be voting against this terrible capitalist plot! I cannot now remember which way I voted, except that I walked backwards and forwards to the polling station, unable to make up my mind. It made me think. It was the start of my realisation that the Labour Party was not the place for me, and that its basic philosophy was flawed.

I subsequently found a home, where I felt comfortable, in the SDP and thereafter in the Liberal Democrats. Above all, I have our Party to thank for meeting my husband Stewart and, of course, he being a Liberal and I from the SDP, we formed our own Alliance!

Diana Wallis has fought two Euro-elections and one general election; is presently a county councillor on Humberside and a councillor on the new unitary East Riding of Yorkshire Council (Deputy Leader of the Liberal Democrat group); PPC for the new constituency of Haltemprice and Howden. In her spare time she is a solicitor.

GRAHAM WATSON MEP

My political consciousness developed between 1970 and 1974. Ted Heath's Government tried two socioeconomic models. I felt neither was right, but distinctly preferred the one after Selsdon. My belief in social consensus extends to employee ownership of industry, an idea too radical for the Labour Party. The idea gained currency in Portugal during the 1974 'carnation revolution', an event which fascinated me. It was the Liberal Party, in the 1977–78 Lib–Lab agreement, which first introduced legislation for employee share ownership plans in the UK.

Economic policy choices dominated western political debate throughout these years, but I came to think of myself as a Liberal – and to join first the YLs (1972) and then the Liberal Party (1974) – for three other reasons: racial equality, concern for the environment and relations with our neighbours on the continent.

Travelling abroad as the son of a Royal Naval officer had made me aware of and profoundly opposed to racial discrimination. The Young Liberals captured my imagination with their active opposition to sporting links with South Africa. (I was never keen on cricket, and disfiguring pitches seemed a powerful non-violent form of protest.)

I found much good sense in EF Schumacher's *Small is Beautiful*. The Liberal Party was at that time the only political party putting forward new ideas about promoting and measuring well-being. My only period of disillusion with the Party came in the mid-1980s, when the Alliance with the SDP blunted our radical cutting edge on environmental policy and allowed the Green Party to emerge.

I was born in March 1956, at the height of the Suez crisis. I grew up in Britain's post-empire, searching-for-a-role generation, and saw Britain's future as a middle-ranking power anchored firmly in the community of western European nations. I questioned the curious but surprisingly resilient assumption that the English Channel was wider than the Atlantic. Heath's advocacy of British membership of the 'Common Market', though laudable and brave, seemed patrician and devoid of idealism. The Liberal Party had argued consistently in favour of European Union, however unpopular,

Being the first Liberal Democrat ever elected to the European Parliament from the UK has therefore been a source of considerable satisfaction; though a liberal can never be long satisfied.

Graham Watson was Head of David Steel's private office 1983–87. He was elected MEP for Somerset and North Devon in 1994.

CLLR DAVID WILLIAMS

TV and radio interviews are not difficult, usually. You are asked questions you have answered many times before. There are several ways to be politely evasive when you don't want to be put on the spot. It was very different in an interview with Ed Boyle for BBC TV in 1991 when he suddenly said: 'I am a Martian, Mr Williams. What is a Liberal Democrat, please?' At least everyone who reads this book will have some chance of producing a coherent answer if they are put on the spot like this.

My reply, with brain in overdrive for a few seconds, was: 'A Liberal Democrat is somebody that really puts people first, that holds to concepts like liberty and freedom, and, I think, in terms of basic politics doesn't see power as an end in itself.'

This instant definition does encapsulate a lot of what attracted me, while still at school, to the Liberal Party in 1957. In essence there are four strands to my allegiance to liberalism and the Liberal Democrats.

Firstly, I have to support the 'party of progress' rather than the 'party of order'. This means being left of centre, and essentially being a liberal, not a conservative.

Secondly, the Liberal Democrats believe in a classless society, as did the Liberal Party, still a radical stance in a class-obsessed Britain.

Thirdly, liberals have a fierce commitment to fairness, freedom, justice and liberty, combined with a proud history of fighting prejudice.

And fourthly, very important for me as a local councillor, Liberal Democrats genuinely believe in the devolution of power, so that government is as close to the people as possible. From this principle we believe in empowerment of people and communities to run their own lives. We believe in sovereignty of the people, not the sovereignty of the Crown in Parliament, or similar old-fashioned rubbish.

Gladstone's most memorable quotation, which I have used in debates on open government and on empowerment, was his contribution to Andrew Reid's 1885 book, *Why I Am a Liberal.* This was a bit of a cheat, as it came from a speech at Chester twenty years earlier. But you can read it on his statue at the National Liberal Club. So next time you pass Mr Gladstone there, reflect on the fact that he understood some of the eternal truths of politics. 'The principle of liberalism is trust in the people, qualified by prudence. The principle of Toryism is mistrust of the people, qualified by fear'.

David Williams is Leader of Richmond upon Thames Council, and Leader of the Opposition on the Association of Metropolitan Authorities.

PART II

Extracts from:

WHY I AM A LIBERAL:

Being Definitions and Personal Confessions of Faith by the Best Minds in the Liberal Party –

collected and edited by
ANDREW REID

published by
CASSELL & CO., 1885

ROBERT BROWNING

Why? Because all I haply can and do,
All that I am now, all I hope to be, -
Whence comes it save from fortune setting free
Body and soul the purpose to pursue,
God traced for both? If fetters, not a few,
Of prejudice, convention, fall from me,
These shall I bid men – each in his degree
Also God-guided – bear, and gaily too?

But little do or can the best of us:
That Little is Achieved Through Liberty.
Who, then, dares hold – emancipated thus -
His fellow shall continue bound? Not I
Who live, love, labour freely, nor discuss
A brother's right to freedom. That is 'Why.'

Robert Browning (1812–89): poet and playwright.

RT HON. W.E. GLADSTONE MP

The principle of liberalism is trust in the people, qualified by prudence: The principle of conservatism is mistrust of the people, qualified by fear.

William Ewart Gladstone (1809–98): Chancellor of the Exchequer, 1852–55, 1859–66. Leader of Commons, 1865–66. Prime Minister, 1868–74. Retired from Liberal leadership 1875, resumed 1880. Prime Minister, 1880–85, 1886, 1892–94.

RT HON. THE EARL OF ROSEBERY

Because I wish to be associated with the best men in the best work.

Arnold Philip Primrose, 5th Earl of Rosebery (1847–1929): Lord Privy Seal, 1885; Chief Commissioner of Works, 1885; Secretary for Foreign Affairs, 1886 and 1892–94; Chairman, London County Council, 1889–90 and 1892; Prime Minster, 1894–95.

RT HON. J. CHAMBERLAIN MP

Progress is the law of the world; and liberalism is the expression of this law in politics.

Through its agency we have gained all that free men may justly prize in our existing institutions, and to it we look for the further changes that will bring them into complete harmony with the needs and aspirations of the people.

True liberalism seeks constantly the greatest happiness of the greatest number, and will attain its end through the wise cooperation of a self-governed commonwealth.

Joseph Chamberlain (1836–1914): Mayor of Birmingham, 1873–76; President Board of Trade, 1880–85; President Local Government Board, 1886. Led Liberal Unionist split from Liberal Party in 1886.

JOSEPH ARCH

Because it was by men like Richard Cobden, John Bright, and other true Liberals, that I as a working man am able to obtain a cheap loaf to feed my family with.

Because the true spirit of liberalism means to give to every man his just rights as a citizen, hence the enfranchisement of 2,000,000 of working men.

I am a Liberal because, when the reform of our Land Laws is dealt with, I have every confidence that a Liberal Government will deal with those laws in the interest of the whole community, and not for the benefit of a privileged few.

It has been the true Liberals who in days gone by have conferred large blessings on the people of this country; their past service for the good of mankind generally has established my confidence in them, that in the future they will confer upon the nation greater freedom by just, wise, and Liberal legislation.

Joseph Arch (1826–1919): founder and leader of National Agricultural Labourers' Union.

ARTHUR ARNOLD MP

Liberalism is the political expression of civilisation; the increase of civil rights; the sharing with others the liberties, the franchises, the privileges, which admit of equal and permanent distribution.

It abhors inequality before the law; it seeks to make legislation respected because of its utility and beneficence.

It ever points to the attainment of happiness and comfort as the result of individual effort; and its cardinal doctrine is that those conditions will be most widely enjoyed where the people are instructed, where the avenues to eminence and usefulness are free and open, where the laws are loved because they are the self-made, and the well-accepted obligations of a wise and contented nation.

Arthur Arnold (1833–1902): President, Free Land League; Chairman, London County Council, 1895–97; knighted 1895.

FRANCIS BENNOCH

.... With the knowledge that on arriving at manhood I could not in England exercise any civil right, because I was a Dissenter, how could I do otherwise than hate the Tory? or how could I help revering the party who struck off my chains of disability, and made me free? ....

REV. LLEWELYN D. BEVAN LL.B. D.D.

.... Liberalism is gathered up in one word – Equality; and this seems to be the essential element of the Christian idea. In the individual relation of man to God, every man stands upon the same foundation. There is one law and one salvation. Hence monarchy and oligarchy, as forms of government, unless they finally rest upon the will of the people, are unchristian. Democracy, which must be the final goal of liberalism, is deducible from the principles of Christianity and the true conception of the Church; and I can only cease to be a Liberal by denying my faith and giving up my Christianity. ....

.... The supreme sanctions, therefore, ofliberalism, as I conceive them, are the interests and welfare of all men, without distinction of race, language, or colour. ....

.... By liberalism, therefore, I understand those principles and that practice which aim, first, at rendering the individual a self-governing person. (This I believe can only be fully accomplished by the method of Jesus, which was the moral rehabilitation and perfecting of each man.) Second, combining men for the common purposes of social life, in such communities as can practically act together, under the necessary limitations of space and time. Third, recognising the unity and solidarity of the entire race. All other conceptions of life seem to me to be pagan and inhuman; to be got rid of as soon as may be, by the methods of thoughtful discourse, persistent teaching, social and political reform – the bloodless revolutions in which alone true liberalism can take part.

Llewelyn Bevan (1842–1918): Vice President, International Congregational Union, 1891; President, Parliamentary Commission on Inebriety, 1901; Chaplain of the Forces, Victoria (Australia).

LADY BRASSEY

From a sincere conviction that true liberalism, not confined only to politics, but carried into all the numerous phases of every-day life, is the only plan by which our social and political order can be effectually sustained. The true Liberal looks not to the interests of certain privileged classes alone, but to those of the community at large. He seeks to promote the greatest happiness of the greatest number by giving freedom of thought and action to all, by extending the means of education, and thus enabling all classes to improve the talents committed to their care, and to appreciate and use wisely, for the elevation of mankind, the privileges which have been conferred upon them through Liberal legislation and government.

HENRY BROADHURST MP

I am a Liberal because the true, full and free application of Liberal principles is best calculated to promote the highest order of manhood. It teaches self-reliance, and gives the best opportunities to the people to promote their individual as well as their united and best permanent interest.

Liberalism does not seek to make all men equal: nothing can do that. But its object is to remove all obstacles erected by men, which prevent all having equal opportunities. This in its turn promotes industry, and makes the realisation of reasonably ambitious hopes possible to the poorest man amongst us.

Henry Broadhurst (1840–1911): Parliamentary Secretary, TUC, 1875–90; Under Secretary, Home Office, 1886 – the first working man in British government.

THOMAS CATLING

.... In the provincial newspaper office where I learned my first political lessons, a printer who had dared to vote for a Liberal was fiercely challenged by his Tory employer. When the man ventured to say that he had voted according his conscience, he was met with the rejoinder, 'D--n your conscience!' and summarily dismissed. The incident is significant, because it represents a principle – the despotic claim of one class to override the feelings and opinions of others. Against such straitened views it is the province of liberalism to wage constant battle. Free trade, a free press, the free expression of opinion, and all our social and religious liberties, have been won by beating down the narrow conservatism which so long barred the way. Wider avenues are now opening, and it is because of my earnest belief that legislation may do much to brighten the lot of the humblest workers, that I desire the triumph of the Liberal cause, which means progress, the growth of freedom, and the advancement of the general good.

Thomas Catling (1838–1920): Editor, Lloyd's Weekly London News, *1884–1907; President, British International Association of Journalists.*

MILLICENT GARRETT FAWCETT

I am a Liberal, because liberalism seems to me to mean faith in the people, and confidence that they will manage their own affairs far better than those affairs are likely to be managed for them by others.

No section of the people has ever been excluded from political power without suffering legislative injustice. To mention only a few instances: the working classes suffered for centuries from laws which attempted to fix the rate of wages, to prevent labourers migrating from place to place in search of better-paid employment, to suppress trade societies, and to facilitate the embezzlement of their funds. Women have suffered, and are still suffering, from a number of unjust laws. A mother, if she is married, has no right to the guardianship of her children, and no right, after they have passed an early age, even to be with them. If her husband is unfaithful to her, the law gives her no claim to a divorce, although infidelity on her part gives her husband the power to put her away. The laws relating to the various cases of intestacy are curious in their consistent injustice to the female relatives, as compared with the male relatives, of the deceased person.

Every case of injustice is a double curse, harming those it is supposed to favour, as much as those to whom it is obviously oppressive; and liberalism, notwithstanding the timidity of some faint-hearted and weak-kneed Liberals, is in the main the force in the political world which cuts at the root of injustice; not so much by tinkering and patching up particular instances of wrong, but by giving the people the power to protect themselves. Equal justice to all, man or woman, workman or aristocrat, is the only sort of liberalism that deserves the name. The liberalism that wishes to exclude half the human race from the benefits arising from liberty and self-government, may make use of sounding phrases, but it is not genuine liberalism, and in time it will meet with the fate that all shams deserve.

Millicent Garrett Fawcett (1847–1929): suffragette; led National Union of Women's Suffrage Societies; educational reformer; founded Newnham College, Cambridge, in 1871.

RT HON. LORD GREVILLE

The history of England proves that the people of its country are its governors. The people cannot be Tory, for the Tory Party only moves when forced for the sake of holding office, or for their own individual benefit, or when a great man, like Lord Beaconsfield, after much labour educates his party, but the education is only given and received for a given purpose, like beings who swallow a bitter medicine. The policy that guides the Tories is in opposition to all Liberal measures; it vilifies statesmen like Gladstone, Bright and Chamberlain; but when by accident they find themselves in power, they meekly take up measures which they had before opposed, but now are forced to adopt if they wish to retain the reins of power.

Liberal measures have given freedom of speech and action. The monarch, the peer, the commoner, the manufacturer, all feel its power; but that power is not the power of the autocrat, it is the gentle breath of liberty given to us Britons by the Liberal Party, which exists, and must ever continue to exist, by the absolute independence of a free, loyal, and law-abiding people.

Lord Greville (1841–1910): Lord of Treasury, 1873–74; Groom-in-Waiting to Queen Victoria, 1868–73.

REV. NEWMAN HALL LL.B.

I am a Liberal because I am Conservative. It is better to repair a house and so uphold it than let it go to ruin by leaving things as they are. The broader the basis of the throne in the extension of popular liberty, the more stable that throne will be. Progressive legislation prompted by justice is safer than legislation yielded to clamour, which it is often too late to still. A foreign policy of justice and conciliation is more likely that one of provocation and aggression to conserve the interests and honour of our country. These are the principles of liberalism, and, therefore, as a Conservative, I support the Liberal Party.

Newman Hall (1816–1902): Chairman, Congregational Union, 1866; founder of Christ Church, Lambeth, 1876.

REV. JOHN PAGE HOPPS

.... The true Liberal, therefore, is opposed to monopoly and privilege, to legislation on behalf of vested interests, to the burdening of the many for the advantaging of the few. He is not an iconoclast, but seeks as his one object to merge all classes and conditions of men into one united whole, with equal social, political, and religious rights for all. ....

John Page Hopps (1834–1911): Baptist Minister; Editor, The Coming Day; *member of first School Board of Glasgow.*

CHARLES H. HOPWOOD QC MP

.... Its watchword is justice; justice to all, high or low, rich or poor. From this flow freedom of opinion, liberty of person, equal political rights at home, manful but conciliatory bearings to the nations abroad. Where so many duties present themselves we must make a choice. The happiness of the population, the prosperity of the country and its sons beyond the seas, demand our first care. Interference in foreign affairs, costly, disastrous, unjust, productive of vainglory, delaying the solution of home questions, has taught us by its results that the truest interests and the real honour of the nation are not served by boastful language, or bloated armaments.

JAMES HOWARD MP

.... I soon discovered an essential difference between Toryism and Liberalism. I perceived that the habit of the Tory Party was to resist changes as long as possible; that their practice was not to argue questions upon their merits, but to appeal to people's fears and prejudices; and that the privileges of particular classes of the community were invariably upheld. On the other hand, the habit of the Liberal Party was to advocate reforms as soon as convinced of their desirableness; to reasons strictly upon the merits of a case; and instead of upholding the exclusive rights and privileges of a class, to advocate their extension to others when justly entitled to them.

A. TAYLOR INNES

I am a Liberal because I am a Scotchman. .... In the history of my own country I find something deeper than the thin stream of its Conservative tradition. I find there in every age a passion for the ideal, and a sense of the obligation of men who deal with public affairs to build upon nothing less than principles of right. And as time goes on, Scotland has fallen back more and more upon such principles – principles of individual freedom, no doubt, but of individual freedom to unite in construction and reconstruction, and so to join with the new principles of Toleration the old passion for truth and right. ....

Alexander Taylor Innes (1833–1912): Advocate-Depute in Scotland.

SIR JOHN LUBBOCK BART. MP

.... I have been a Liberal because the Liberal Party has been contending for principles now generally admitted to be of great national advantage, and among the most important of which may be mentioned civil and religious liberty, peace abroad, economy at home, freedom of trade, a fairer distribution of seats, the extension of the franchise, and last, but not least, the general education of the people. .... As regards the future, I trust that parliament will alter the law, so as to promote, instead of discouraging, small holdings; to facilitate the transfer of land; to improve our system of education; to limit generally, as well as in factories, the hours of labour of young persons; to increase the number of free libraries; to improve our system of local government; etc. ....

Sir John Lubbock (1834–1913): Vice Chancellor, London University, 1874–80; introduced bank holidays (1871); created 1st Earl of Avebury, 1900.

P. STEWART MACLIVER MP

Because to liberalism we owe the removal of the taxes on knowledge, which has given to England a Free Press, has provided cheap literature, and has made our newspapers powerful agencies in the education of the people in religion and morality.

RT HON. GEORGE OSBORNE MORGAN QC MP

I am a Liberal because I prefer progress to stagnation; because I place the happiness of the many above the privileges of the few; and because I believe that disastrous revolutions are best averted by timely reforms.

George Osborne Morgan (1826–97): Chairman, Welsh Liberal MPs; Judge-Advocate-General, 1880–85; Parliamentary Secretary to the Colonies, 1886; introduced Burials Act, 1880, Married Women's Property Act, 1882, Act abolishing corporal punishment in the Army.

GEORGE W.E. RUSSELL MP

Liberalism has already secured us personal and political liberty; freedom of thought; and merciful laws.

For the future, liberalism offers us an honest policy abroad, which means the avoidance of the most terrible of all evils – unnecessary war. Liberalism is loyal to Free Trade, which alone insures abundance of food in the homes of those who earn it by daily labour. Liberalism is pledged to a steady perseverance in social reform, and thereby guarantees us against communism and revolution.

George Russell (1853–1919): Parliamentary Secretary, Local Government Board, 1883–85; Under-Secretary of State for India, 1892–94, for Home Department, 1894–95; Chairman, Churchmen's Liberation League.

RT HON. G.J. SHAW-LEFEVRE MP

Liberalism aims at a higher standard of happiness, in its widest and best sense, for the people as a whole. It is necessarily progressive, for its aims advance as it succeeds in approaching them.

In domestic legislation it prefers the interests of the nation to those of any section or class of it, while it endeavours to secure its objects without doing wrong or injustice to individuals.

Its principles are not less important in their practical application by authorities, from whatever source they may derive their power. It prescribes that, without regard to the accidents of birth or wealth, or to differences of religious of other opinions, all men are entitled to equal treatment and equal justice.

In foreign affairs it holds that the interests of our country can never be concerned in the maintenance of oppression or injustice in any part of the world; and that the highest maxim for our guidance in our relations to other nations is 'to do to others as we would they should do to us.'

GEORGE R. SIMS

Why am I a Liberal? Because I believe that a Liberal policy promotes the happiness of the people; because liberalism means the greatest good of the greatest number; because it concerns itself with the rights and wrongs of the many, as opposed to conservatism, which concerns itself only with the rights and wrongs of the few; because I would rather march as a cheerful pioneer towards the goal of Freedom, than be dragged along a sullen captive in the rear of the advancing and victorious army; because the watchwords of the true Liberal are justice, liberty, and progress; and I can find no better in the English language.

George R. Sims (1847–1922): journalist and dramatic author; Knight of the Royal Norwegian Order of St Olaf, first class, 1905.

DR WALTER SMITH

.... Conservatism, indeed, has its use in the State. It helps to slow the course of progress till there has been sufficient deliberation and discussion. So a brake is a good thing; but a locomotive is better. .... The Liberal Party, then, has all along its history been identified with the improvement of our national institutions – with broader franchises, the abolition of monopolies, the equalisation of taxes, freedom of opinion, and with all other measures which are now generally recognised as stages of our national progress. .... I am a Liberal, then, because I regard the drift and spirit of their foreign policy as more just than that of their opponents, more in sympathy with the freedom of other peoples, more averse to needless war and bloodshed, more truly religious because more righteous than that of their opponents. ....

Walter Smith (1844–1932): President, Royal Academy of Medicine, Ireland; Presdent, Royal College of Physicians, Ireland, 1892–95.

RT HON. JAMES STANSFELD MP

Liberalism believes in individuality, in the capacity for liberty and progress of the individual man. .... But though party organisation necessarily restricts individual freedom of political action, it is least able to be coercive amongst true Liberals, with whom respect for individuality, a strong sense, in their own persons, of its rights, coupled with a distaste for exaggerated disciplinary coercion, have become a second nature.

Accordingly, the formation of a Liberal Party is necessarily of a looser order than that of conservatism; and this is a cause to Liberals of satisfaction, an evidence that their party remains faithful to its true character, and an assurance of its health and vigour. ....

Sir James Stansfeld (1820–98): Lord of Treasury 1868–69; President Poor Law Board, 1871; President Local Government Board, 1871–74; resigned to devoted himself to securing repeal of Contagious Diseases Acts; resumed office 1886.

RT HON. LORD THURLOW

.... If it is said that any of these things are Radical doctrines, then the Liberal is a Radical; and, for my own part, I know of no distinction between the two except in name, and in the degree of fear, envy, hatred, malice, and all uncharitableness which the one or the other of these synonymous appellations engenders in the Conservative breast.

Lord Thurlow (1838–1916): diplomat (served on Earl of Elgin's mission to China, 1860–61): Paymaster-General, 1886; Lord High Commissioner of General Assembly of Church of Scotland, 1886.

WILLIAM VOLCKMAN

Radicals have been aptly described as 'Liberals in earnest.' .... Because, then, there are monopolies to reduce, oppressions to disestablish, wrongs to remedy; because poverty must be brought within the range of curative and preventive agencies; and because, to that end, some of the principles of well-being have still to be sought out, and others more effectually applied, there are reasons enough and to spared for being a Liberal – for cultivating those progressive tendencies which are finding their fullest expression in Radicalism.

ALFRED RUSSEL WALLACE LL.D.

.... Although very slow to act upon its convictions, the Liberal Party recognises fundamental principles as a basis of reform, and aims at unbought justice and equal freedom for all as the ultimate goal of political progress. ....

Alfred Russel Wallace (1823–1913): author, explorer and scientist (published Natural Selection, *1870); President, Land Nationalisation Society.*

WHY I AM A LIBERAL: AN ESSAY BY ANDREW REID

Chapter I: An Ideal Liberal

In defining an ideal Liberal, I think the first feature we shall know him by is this: he will love the approval of his own conscience more than the approval of the conscience of the people. He will prefer to the applause of the multitude the still small voice within him, acknowledging him in the right. ....

He will be a man of profound simplicity of force; who carries his countrymen with him not by any tricks or devices for manufacturing popularity and advertising himself, but by the solidity and directness of his methods and purpose. ....

The ideal Liberal will be a teacher and prophet among the people. It is significant, but it is true, that a Tory is never a teacher or prophet of the multitude. ....

He will be a just man. If he appeals for justice for the weak, in the hearing of the strong, he will not change his voice in the hearing of the poor, and become the advocate of injustice towards the rich. ....

He will be the liberator of the hamlet and so the liberator of his country; he will be the saviour of the village, and so the saviour of the nation; he will be the reformer of the hearth, and so the reformer of the world. He is the eye of the oppressed, the voice of the weak, the hand of the struggling. ....

The man whose feet stand on a rock, whose foundations of political principles is solid, and high as it is solid, whose hope, faith and sympathy are as boundless and yet as practical and useful to man as the light, is an ideal Liberal. ....

He is a man of indestructible, illimitable, and indomitable faith. ....

The ideal Liberal will exercise boundless charity towards all opinion, even towards those which are thought bad. ....

He will be a man, I repeat, of unlimited charity. He will not think his country must be in the right because it is his country; or his opinions must be in the right because they are his opinions; or his party in the right because it is his party; or his own conscience in the right because it is his conscience. ....

The ideal Liberal is a modern man and a scientific man. He does not dwell in the present and live in the past; rather he dwells in the present but lives in the future. .... He has no idea of finality. He refuses to listen to the voice of the darkness – 'thus far shalt thou come and no farther'. ....

He is a modern man. He looks into the face of change as a child looks into the face of his father. He sees nothing of which to be afraid. ....Change! It is the law which discovers for him those institutions which have the element of decay and of finality; it is the law which limits the rights and the functions of the past over the present; it is the law which submits the present to the reign of the future. It is the principle of growth, and continuity of progress, as opposed to riot, disorder, violent revolution. It is the principle of gradual, continuous, incessant movement, as distinguished from stagnation, decay, extinction on the one hand, or reckless leaps into the dark on the other. ....

An ideal Liberal is a Foundation Man. .... he builds his structure of reform upon the solid ground, and not upon artificial foundations. .... He does not build the structure of society with laws, but with principles. 'One principle,' he says, 'is worth a hundred laws.' .... He observes 'the greatest political cry we ever had was 'Repeal,' and the greatest cry we can still have,' he declares, is "Repeal." And then after we have carted away this rubbish of laws, we shall have cleared the ground for a magnificent site upon which, on a few simple principles, each man can build himself without laws.

The ideal Liberal is a Whole Liberal. .... He is sound all over and thorough right through.

Lastly, crowning all, and greatest of all, an ideal Liberal is a Man. He pays homage to Man. He inculcates within him a love and reverence for Man. To him no institutions are so ancient, so noble, so beautiful as Man.

It is the temple of God within which he worships, and he knows no religion greater than the political faith which would teach him that the true worship of the father is to love man and to do his duty to his brother. It is a lofty liberalism, such as he yearns humbly to follow. It points him to some distant future of society so beautiful and happy that no tongue shall be able to describe it, much less we, at this far-off distance, imagine it.

PART III

WHY ARE WE LIBERAL DEMOCRATS?

DUNCAN BRACK

So why are we Liberal Democrats? One contributor told me he thought he'd probably forgotten; he'd been one for so long it was now simply a matter of habit. But in his contribution, along with all the others', you will find themes and patterns which recur time and again – and can often be linked back to those which featured in the statements of the Liberals of 1885. These pages offer a brief guide.

First impressions

As many contributors pointed out, what initially attracts an individual to the Party is not necessarily what keeps them in. But it is important.

One name recurs time after time in the pieces of those aged 45 and over: Jo Grimond. Grimond's idealism, his imagination, his ability to communicate, his *freshness,* were clearly of central importance to the postwar revival of the Liberal Party – more so, I suspect, than many of us too young to remember him as leader realise. Liberal opposition to the Suez adventure is another recurring feature, attracting many to the Party in opposition to Conservative imperialism and Labour equivocation. The foundation of the SDP, and, amongst the younger and newer Party members, the leadership of Paddy Ashdown, has also helped attract support and converted passive adherence into active commitment.

A general common factor is disgust with the alternatives on offer – particularly with the Conservatives. The Labour Party is seen in a marginally more favourable light. 'One wanted to believe that its heart was in the right place,' explained one contributor, 'but it housed so many crabbed zealots and unattractive bullies that such a leap of faith was impossible.' Labour's record in local government, its too-close links with the unions, and, most recently, its apparent lack of principle, are all powerful negative features.

Policies

Specific policy proposals feature occasionally – more frequently, in general, amongst those contributors who are Party sympathisers rather than activists. The most common policy mentioned is support for electoral reform, seen as the way to restore sanity and balance to a political system comprehensively failing the country. The Liberal Democrat position on Europe ranks close behind – hardly surprising, given current political circumstances – with federalism and decentralisation also featuring strongly. Investment in education and, particularly for Grimond-era converts, worker participation, are also often mentioned.

Style

Leadership, lack of alternatives, and specific policy positions may help gain attention and votes, but much more is needed to win wholehearted commitment and belonging. The *style* of the Liberal Democrats is more important in this respect. The Party is seen as:

Pluralist: aware it has no monopoly of wisdom, not afraid to work with others, and seeking cooperation rather than confrontation;
Independent: free of vested interests, and especially of any class bias (a very strong link to the Liberals of 1885);
Participatory: in its internal organisation, particularly in policy-making;
Honest: not afraid to put forward unpopular policies;
Thoughtful: not dogmatic;
Anarchic: disrespectful of authority, and difficult to discipline; and
On the side of the individual: against the state, big business, organised labour – the big battalions of today's society.

Being honest, of course, a number of the contributors are also aware of the Party's failings. The Liberal Democrat emphasis on localism, in many ways one of its strengths, has its negative side: an obsession with local populism and local roots above all else. Most commonly, the Party is criticised for its lack of radicalism, 'of trying too hard to look like a government (or opposition) in waiting,' rather than having the courage of its convictions. Some things never change – a number of the 1885 contributors had much the same criticism.

Philosophy

But it is the Liberal Democrat *philosophy* – its underlying beliefs, values and assumptions – that is the key to understanding what makes the Party tick, and also what makes it different. Here the similarities with the Liberals of 1885 are most marked, for those who came into the present-day Party from the SDP as well as for those from the Liberal Party.

Liberal Democrats start from an optimistic view of human nature: 'an idealism about the human spirit, the capacity of humans to do good;'

'despite all the horrid evidence to the contrary, persuaded of the hope of humanity.' The purpose of politics is the construction of a society in which the infinite possibilities of the individual can be realised. 'Our aim is not the perpetuation or perfection of this or that mechanism or system, but that individual men and women may have life, and may have it more abundantly.'

Therefore *liberty* is the goal of political systems, and the central political issue is the structure of the institutions through which power is exercised. 'The biggest and most important challenge for Liberal Democrats is to stop concentrations and abuses of power.' The Party shares a general distrust of institutions – even when they are run by Liberal Democrats – and of authority, tradition, and 'received wisdom'. It aims to construct systems in which individuals are free to be different, through which they are enabled and encouraged to take and to use power for themselves. 'Give them some power to change their lives and they do not abuse it but use it sensitively for the general good.' Where power must be exercised through institutions, they must be as open, as democratic, as participatory and as near to the people they serve as possible.

In achieving these objectives, the key task for Liberal Democrats is to ensure that 'no-one shall be enslaved by poverty, ignorance or conformity,' the section of the preamble to the Party constitution most frequently quoted by contributors.

As one pointed out, many political creeds oppose poverty, but only Liberal Democrats express this belief in terms of liberty. 'Poverty prevents people from being free – free to make choices and even, when the struggle just to survive is paramount, to think their own thoughts.' Therefore the Party campaigns for justice, for rights to basic services and for structures of society and community which are inclusive, which ensure that no-one is excluded because of ill health, or disability, or lack of opportunity, or lack of self-confidence. For Liberal Democrats, emphatically there *is* such as thing as society.

A market-based economy is clearly preferred to intervention and regulation (though Liberal Democracy is not, unlike many other political philosophies, driven primarily by economic analysis), but equally there is an important role for a strong public sector. And poverty is not seen in a purely material sense. Freedom from the poverty of a degraded environment is a constant theme, and the green credentials of the Party, reinforced by its stress on the need for government to think long term, one of its most distinctive characteristics.

Freedom from ignorance underpins Liberal Democrat proposals to invest in education, and also, perhaps more importantly, to a commitment to rational and informed debate and decision. Ignorance excludes people from society and government just as surely as poverty. Hence the Liberal Democrat hatred of bigotry, prejudice and intolerance.

Freedom from conformity follows naturally from these beliefs, and perhaps derives most directly from the Victorian Liberalism of John Stuart Mill, who devoted the bulk of his famous essay *On Liberty* to an assault on society's pressures to conform. 'Human creativity is the ultimate resource, and its shackling by convention and prejudice the ultimate extravagance.' A commitment to civil liberties, to a framework of laws and rights which ensures individuals are free to be themselves, as long as they do not impose their views on others, follows naturally.

Finally – a point picked up by many, many contributors – Liberal Democrats are internationalists. The negative aspects of the nation state embody many of the characteristics that are anathema to the Party: xenophobia, intolerance, racism. Cooperation rather than confrontation must be the norm for nations as much as individuals, particularly in tackling the major global problems of the twenty-first century. And the completion of the European federalist enterprise is one of the Party's most cherished objectives.

Conclusion

No doubt none of those whose pieces have been included in this book would agree completely with this brief analysis. Indeed, there can hardly be such a thing as an authoritative version of what it is to be a Liberal Democrat; the experience and the beliefs are too personal and individual.

It hardly matters. If this book has helped to explain to those outside the Party why we are Liberal Democrats; to have indicated the continuities in the philosophies of those who called themselves Liberals in 1885 and those who call themselves Liberal Democrats now; and, perhaps, to have encouraged the latter to question and refine their own beliefs; then it will have served its cause.